MODERN VERSION FAILURES

MODERN VERSION FAILURES

Published by
THE BIBLE FOR TODAY PRESS
900 Park Avenue
Collingswood, New Jersey 08108
U.S.A.
Pastor D. A. Waite, Th.D., Ph.D.
𝔅𝔦𝔟𝔩𝔢 𝔉𝔬𝔯 𝔗𝔬𝔡𝔞𝔶 𝔅𝔞𝔭𝔱𝔦𝔰𝔱 𝔆𝔥𝔲𝔯𝔠𝔥
Church Phone: 856-854-4747
BFT Phone: 856-854-4452
Orders: 1-800-John 10:9
e-mail: BFT@BibleForToday.org
Website: www.BibleForToday.org
Fax: 856-854-2464

We Use and Defend
The King James Bible

February, 2014
BFT 4085
Copyright, 2014
All Rights Reserved
ISBN #978-1-56848-097-8

Cover Design and Publishing facilitated by:
The Old Paths Publications, Inc.
www.theoldpathspublications.com
706-865-0153

FOREWORD

The Author. Charles Kriessman has had an interest in the subject of the Bible versions for many years, but especially since the year 2000. He was born in Washington, D.C. sixty-three years ago. He attended Gustavus Adolphus College in St. Peter, MN, and Orange Coast College in Costa Mesa, CA. He holds an Associate degree in Religious Education and a Bachelor of Theology degree. He is presently working on a Masters degree.

The Plan. The author has chosen for the subject of the book *Modern Version Failures*. He has developed this subject in seven brief chapters: (1) Casting Down Imaginations; (2) The Whole Armor of God; (3) Truth; (4) Our Battleground; (5) Inspiration; (6) Preservation; and (7) Failure Alert.

The Appendices. To further elaborate on the main theme of the book, the author has three Appendices: (1) Some Words About Peter Ruckman; (2) The Textus Receptus; and (3) Doctrinal Fruit.

The Editor And Publisher. The author asked The Bible For Today to assist him in the production of this book. Therefore, I have made some editions and put it in the format for publication.

D. A. Waite

Pastor D. A. Waite, Th.D., Ph.D.
Director of the **Bible For Today**, Incorporated, and
Pastor of the 𝕭ible 𝕱or 𝕿oday 𝕭aptist 𝕮hurch

TABLE OF CONTENTS

Chapter Titles   **Page**

INTRODUCTION

This is a paper that reiterates that the King James Bible is considered superior to all modern versions. In his book, *Defending the King James Bible*, Dr. D.A. Waite states four superiorities why this is so. The King James Bible has: 1) superior texts, 2) superior translators, 3) superior translation technique, and 4) superior theology.

It is a raging battle over the Words in our Bible. What are the Old Testament Words in Hebrew and Aramaic that came to us from God? Which are the New Testament Words in Greek? The underlying Words which were preserved and translated into our King James Bible will be put forth as the true Words which we have today.

Modern versions today use a different group of Hebrew, Aramaic, and Greek Words. Different and questionable translation techniques are employed. The result of these translation techniques is a process of change, of dynamics which does not carry over the Words of the original language into the words of another language.

The end result is that the theology of the modern versions, because of inferior texts, techniques, and translators, suffers greatly. Although denied, doctrinal changes arise from Gnostic Greek texts being in error. This will be dealt with here.

The Dean Burgon Society seeks to defend the King James Bible and its underlying traditional Words. The KJV is to be cherished and used but we must remember that it was translated from the correct Hebrew, Aramaic, and Greek Words. What the Devil and his minions are seeking to do is destroy the King James Bible. Men have perpetuated the use of corrupted Westcott and Hort Greek texts. They have been corrupting the

Hebrew, Aramaic, and Greek from 1881 and before. This is not to continue. The truth has been out there now for decades. Authors such as Dean Burgon, Edward Hills, Moorman, Waite, and others have built on a foundation of truth about the modern Bible version issue. Textual critics and Ruckmanites exhibit an entrenchment in seminaries, major Bible societies and apostate churches.

Their position is weak and indefensible. Their obstinance is strong and obnoxious. There must now be the will to cause upset to the status quo. The battle is for the army of the Lord Jesus Christ to stand and withstand. The Received Text must end up victorious and we must be glorified in the Lord Jesus Christ. This paper is an attempt to equip and move the battle forward in the Lord Jesus Christ.

So, how do you defend a position that the Westcott and Hort, Nestle-Aland (27th ed.), and United Bible Societies (UBS 4ed.) Texts change the Scrivener's Greek New Testament in 5,604 places? According to Dr. D.A. Waite, President of the Dean Burgon Society, of those changes, 35% were omissions, 8% additions, and 57% are changes. 4,366 more words were affected in these 5,604 places, for a total of 9,970 Greek Words that were changed. That would mean, that in Scrivener's Greek text, an average of 15.4 words for every page were changed by the W-H text from the Received Text. This is a 7% or 45.9 page alteration of the Greek Words (See **BFT #1442**). In Dr. Moorman's side by side count in his book, "*Missing in Modern Bibles*," he found that the Nestle-Aland Greek Text used for the modern English versions, were 2,886 Greek words shorter than the Received Text. This is the equivalent, in English words, of omitting the entire books of first and second Peter.

So-called textual scholars then throw up their hands and utter, "what difference at this point does it make?"[1] Despite shoulder-shrugs, it makes a terrible textual difference. It makes a difference in 356 doctrines to be exact, according to Dr. Jack

Moorman. In his book, *Early MSS, Church Fathers, and the Authorized Version* (From Bible for Today Press, Collingswood, NJ) Dr. Moorman chronicled those 356 Doctrinal Errors in the N.I.V. and other modern Bible versions.

Dr. D. A. Waite, in his book, *Defending the King James Bible* presents 158 doctrines that are affected in the modern Bible versions as a result of modern textual critics using corrupted manuscripts Vatican B and Sinaiticus Aleph.

Sixty-five (65) doctrinal failures are presented here. Failure can be so many things: unsuccess, nonsuccess, unfulfillment, nonfulfillment, forlorn hope, miscarriage, misfire, fizzle, flop, crash, fall, etc. The ancient Gnostics failed by mutilating pure Hebrew, Aramaic, and Greek Words. This continued through Westcott and Hort who, as apostates, failed along with the Gnostics in deliberately adding to the failure. What is sad today is the continued slavish attachment to B and Aleph--both failed Greek manuscripts, thoroughly vetted by Dean John William Burgon in *The Revision Revised*.

It is hoped that further exposure of doctrinal failures in today's modern versions will reawaken the Christian world and redirect it away from the failure and error. It is also hoped that this can be viewed as not being "preaching to the choir." The battle and its waging can be learned by all Christians not up to speed with the issues. It may neither be accepted by modern day Gnostics at heart, nor be taken as the jumping-off point from the runaway-false-text-train. That can only be hoped for.

Getting to Heaven

While it may be true that this material is open to all, it is written for the brethren--those believers who know about this version issue or who are curious about it. But it is imperative that a person must be saved, for it is the only way to heaven.

You must realize that you are a sinner and that you need a Saviour. You cannot go to heaven if you die in your sin.

"For all have sinned, and come short of the glory of God" (Romans 3:23).
"The wicked shall be turned into hell,..." (Psalm 9:17a).

Agree with God that you are a sinner and change your mind about sin.

"And the times of this ignorance God winked at; but now commandeth all men everywhere to repent:" (Acts 17:30).

Believe that the Lord Jesus Christ came and took all the punishment for your sins so that you could be made free.

"For I delivered unto you first of all that which I also received, how that Christ died for our sins according to the scriptures; and that he was buried, and that he rose again the third day according to the scriptures:" (1 Corinthians 15:3,4).

Now, you must genuinely believe in and receive the Lord Jesus Christ as your Lord and Saviour.

"For God so loved the world, that he gave his only begotten Son, that whosoever believeth in him should not perish, but have everlasting life" (John 3:16).

"For with the heart man believeth unto righteousness; and with the mouth confession is made unto salvation" (Romans 10:10).

If you have believed unto righteousness and received the Lord Jesus Christ as your Saviour according to the promise in John 3:16, please contact as soon as possible: Pastor D. A. Waite at:

Bible for Today
900 Park Avenue
Collingswood, NJ 08108
856-854-4747
BFT@BibleforToday.org

Some Terms

Autograph--A manuscript of the original text in Hebrew, Aramaic, or Greek.

Apograph--Hand written copy of the original Words.

Apostasy--From the Greek Word *apostasia* meaning "to fall away." Used of a person professing the true faith, but falls away from the faith, revealing an absence of or a failure of obtaining true faith.

Bibliology--The doctrine of the Bible.

Canon--From the Greek *kanon*, meaning a "rule, standard, or measuring rod" which includes all 66 books of the Bible.

Carnal--Fleshly, pertaining to the body or flesh; worldly, or fleshly desires, under the influence of (Romans 7:14; 1 Peter 2:11).

Critical Text (CT)--The Westcott–Hort Greek Text represented today in the Nestle-Aland, UBS 4th ed. Greek Texts; made up of a mere 45 manuscripts, of which two are used as its basis, the Vaticanus (B) and Sinaiticus (Aleph).

Doctrine--Teachings, what is taught, instruction.

Dynamic Equivalence--Translation of the message, thoughts, ideas of groups of Words of the original language. Adding, subtracting, and changing those Words.

Eisegesis--Biblical interpretation where someone's ideas are read into scriptures which is not there.

Exegesis--Analysis of Biblical texts according to literal – grammatical – historical methodology.

Formal Equivalence--Translation that translates, wherever possible, the forms of the original Words into the forms of the language of translation.

Gnosticism--From the Greek Word *gnosis*, meaning "knowledge." Taught in 2nd century that flesh is evil and that the Lord Jesus Christ was a man, not God manifested in the flesh.

Heresy--From the Greek *hairesis*, meaning a "denial of revealed truth, causing destructive opinions."

Higher Criticism--Rejects inspiration of the Bible. Treats Bible Words as being created solely by human beings, putting together the Bible according to human desires, by different authors.

Imaginations--A mental image that is not real to the senses; assumptions, suppositions, conjectures, guesses; lies.

Infallible--Not being capable of error in teachings; authority, word order, etc., the Bible being incapable of error.

Inerrant--Having no errors, usually reserved for the original manuscripts of the Bible.

Inspiration–A word used in the Bible, technical in its meaning and usage, meaning "God-breathed." A miracle by which the Words of the Bible were perfectly given in Hebrew, Aramaic, and Greek. This process was once delivered to mankind, directly from Heaven, recorded perfectly once, Word by Word, all the Words which are infallible and inerrant. These Words make up the Canon of Scripture in the Hebrew Masoretic Text and Greek Textus Receptus.

Liberalism--Takes naturalistic approach to the Bible, denying divine inspiration, preservation, and miracles, elevating the element of rationalism.

Origenism–Based on teachings of Origen, a Gnostic, denied the basic doctrines including inspiration and preservation–one of the first to corrupt true manuscripts.

Perfect Tense--The Greek perfect is the tense of a verb that has an action in the past, which continues in the present and into the future.

Plenary--The "total of" all the Scripture.

Polemic--From the Greek *polemikos*, meaning "warlike." An offensive attack on the theology or beliefs of another.

Received Text (Textus Receptus, TR)--The Greek text, Beza's 5th edition of 1598, which was the text underlying the King James Bible.

Saint--A born-again, Bible believing Christian.

Scripture--The 66 books of the Old and New Testaments. Used in 2 Timothy 3:16 to mean Hebrew and Aramaic copies, and, by extension, the Greek Textus Receptus.

Chapter One
Casting Down Imaginations

4 (For the weapons of our warfare are not carnal, but mighty through God to the pulling down of strongholds;) 5 Casting down imaginations, and every high thing that exalteth itself against the knowledge of God, and bringing into captivity every thought to the obedience of God; 6 And having in a readiness to revenge all disobedience, when your obedience is fulfilled [1] (2 Corinthians 10:4-6).

The casting down of imaginations is such an important command. The doctrinal corruptions found in modern Bible versions, and the exaltation of high things against the Lord Jesus and His saints, must be brought into captivity and obedience to the Lord Jesus Christ.

The meaning of the word imaginations has many variances but one main thread runs through it. The mind can form mental images of things not actually present. That is pretty scary when you think of unsaved minds, in Satan's control, masterminding ways of mis-handling God's sacred Words.

Logismos is the Greek Word for calculations, reckonings, reflections, which translate into high things that are hostile to God's Holy Bible.

> *"The Lord knoweth the thoughts of man, that they are vanity"* (Psalm 94:11).
>
> *"The thoughts of the wicked are an abomination to the Lord: but the words of the pure are pleasant words"* (Proverbs 15:26).

> *"Let the wicked forsake his way, and the*
> *unrighteous man his thoughts: and let him return*
> *unto the Lord, . . .* (Isaiah 55:7a).

What is being taught in the colleges and seminaries about the textual issue are total lies. The thoughts of the hearts of those teaching are only lies. The thoughts of the hearts of the students coming out, are only lies. They and their thoughts are exalting themselves above God. They are lifting their own thoughts and lies above God's truth.

These dark places of learning are the strongholds that must be demolished. The strongholds are in people's minds. They are built by lie upon lie. The Devil is in charge, he is the father of lies. He leads the unwary into sin, he props himself up as bigger than God. He teaches that God cannot be trusted, all the while God is telling us we can trust Him. The Devil wants everyone to exalt themselves now, and not to wait.

There are warnings about the substitution of men's thoughts and intentions in place of God's. God's holy Words reveal such treachery and men are caught in their own web of lies.

> *"Which shew the work of the law written in their*
> *hearts, their conscience also bearing witness,*
> *and their thoughts the mean while accusing or*
> *else excusing one another;"* (Romans 2:15)

Mental images, things made up, imaginings. Isn't that the description of the Critical Text since the true Words were corrupted by the Gnostics? Didn't Origen dream up his corruptions by thinking this is what was meant? This whole time from the 1st century on, apostate men have driven the whole textual issue upon pretext, assumption, and imaginings.

Nearly all unsaved people have exalted their own thoughts above God's thoughts. This is a tragic mistake and not one that will get them anywhere but hell. Many saved people have had God's thoughts supplanted by their own. This is also tragic and will lead to a loss of reward and they will end up being a bad example to other believers.

> *"And whosoever shall exalt himself shall be abased; and he that shall humble himself shall be exalted"* (Matthew 23:12).

The mind is the battlefield. We are up against strongholds. Our Christian life is not going to stop being warfare. If we are victorious in one thing by the grace of God, it does not mean the battle is over. Satan is there at the start of a Christian's life, in the middle and at the end. Satan attacked the Lord Jesus Christ at the beginning of His ministry immediately after He was baptized. Satan attacked all through His ministry up to the cross. We can be confident because the Lord Jesus Christ overcame the world. No matter how hot the battle, our Lord is there with us in the conflict. The Lord Jesus Christ,

> *"Who hath delivered us from the power of darkness, and hath translated us into the kingdom of his dear Son:"* (Colossians 1:13).

We have been taken out of the kingdom of Satan and placed into the kingdom of God. Satan has no power over us; we are under the Lord Jesus Christ's power.

The Battle for the Mind

The key to winning the battle of the mind is the thoughts of the mind and heart. We are to bring into captivity every thought to the obedience of the Lord Jesus Christ. The liberals and modernists wish to control the Words of God. Their behavior needs to be changed. Their thinking and the control by the Devil and his minions over them needs to be broken.

The ones who advocate the modern versions have walls built around their minds and hearts. Satan has built them up brick by brick. Each tenet of perverted doctrine has gone into the laying of each brick. Each lie of the Devil about Critical Text beliefs has strengthened that wall. It has taken hold now over centuries.

What is our challenge then in regards to the textual issue?

We are to keep breaking into those strongholds that exalt man above God. Reduce and isolate the influence of the Westcott and Hort type texts and dump them into the dumpster. Free ourselves of any strongholds that Satan may have started to construct within our minds and hearts. Throw out the lies. Expose them to the light constantly. Use spiritual warfare to defeat the enemy and apply our Lord's intercession.

Guard the Heart

Read God's Words, live the Words, pray without ceasing, rejoice evermore. Keep reading the Words. That's what we are fighting the good fight about. The truth, God's truth. The truth is in the Words of God. The truth is God's Words. The Devil's imaginations are attacking that truth. His lies come against the truth. He substitutes lies for truth. The proof is in the dead seminaries, the Greek departments of evangelical colleges and with the Ruckmanites.

> *"Every imagination of the thoughts of his heart*
> *was only evil continually"* (Genesis 6:5).

Every lie of the heart goes into the building of the wall of strongholds. The words *"Pulling down"* and *"casting down,"* are forms of the same Word in Greek, *Kathaireo*. It is spiritual demolition, the same as the physical demolition or tearing down of old buildings. Everything we know to be lies, should be torn down, and excluded from entering into our soul. Don't keep passing lies along to all that will hear, either verbally or through the printed word. Amongst the brethren, let love and trust abide with the truth and continually be edified.

> *"The grace of our Lord Jesus Christ be with you*
> *all. Amen"* (2 Thessalonians 3:18).

Live the Word

Next, we must live the Words of God. This has been drilled into the brethren over and over. How can one defend something that is not going to apply to our spiritual lives? Reading is good, but we need to guard our minds and hearts, by allowing the Lord Jesus Christ to live in us and through us. Beware of Satan's attacks on our lives. Be strong in spirit, be leaders in our families. Have peace in our lives between spouses and children.

> *"So ought men to love their wives as their own bodies. He that loveth his wife loveth himself"* (Ephesians 5:28).

> *"And ye fathers, provoke not your children to wrath: but bring them up in the nurture and admonition of the Lord"* (Ephesians 6:4).

We must serve and love the Lord *"and walk in love, as Christ also hath loved us"* (Ephesians 5:2a), *"with good will doing service, as to the Lord, and not to men:"* (Ephesians 6:7).

Purify the mind with the thoughts, Words and blessings of our Lord Jesus Christ.

> *"And be not conformed to this world: but be ye transformed by the renewing of your mind, that ye may prove what is that good, and acceptable, and perfect, will of God"* (Romans 12:2).

Purge out, dig out, and ask God to refine those impure things in our minds. Everything that is corrupt must be dug out and refined out of your mind.

> *"And be renewed in the spirit of your mind; And that ye put on the new man, which after God is created in righteousness and true holiness"* (Ephesians 4:23.24).

Purge out imaginations Satan has planted. Get rid of weaknesses, hate, envy, past hurts, bad relationships, and evil concupiscence. Mortify the evil.

> *"Mortify therefore your members which are upon the earth; fornication, uncleanness, inordinate affection, evil concupiscence, and covetousness, which is idolatry:"* (Colossians 3:5).

We can do all things through the Lord Jesus Christ.

Praying Always

We cannot cast or pull down imaginations until we know how to pray.

> "*Praying always with all prayer and supplication in the Spirit, and watching thereunto with all perseverance and supplication for all saints;*" (Ephesians 6:18).

> "*Be careful for nothing; but in everything by prayer and supplication with thanksgiving let your requests be made known unto God*" (Philippians 4:6).

Go to God in prayer. Have close fellowship with the Most High. Bring His power to bear for ourselves, for others who are saved and unsaved. We need the Father to change things and to give us the secret of power and life. We must be alone and quiet with Him in our mind and our spirit. Be knowledgeable of His love to us when He gave us His Son. Glorify Him.

Let His will be done in us, as it is done in Heaven. Pray to advance His truth and His salvation. Be faithful in accepting His love and be obedient to do His will.

As we have needed His forgiveness, being sinners, we owe everything to Him and our forgiveness to the precious Blood that covers us. Pray that we might be able to forgive others and to owe no debt to any man.

Have Him deliver us and protect us from the evil one and his wiles. Pray for God's power and love to keep us from the Tempter's power to ensnare. We need to pray to be in holy obedience to God by the power of the Holy Ghost in us.

Fulfill our Duty

What do we say then? It is our duty as Christian soldiers of the cross to pull down and demolish strongholds. These come as imaginations and we must take a stand against the wiles of the Devil. Practice what we preach, read the Bible, live the Words of God, and pray, pray, pray. Remember that the imaginations of the hearts of men are only evil continually. Guard against this with the tools that the Lord has given us. The Lord Jesus Christ leads the battle. Preach the gospel so that all men may be saved.

Set our eyes upon the Lord and set aside our own thoughts and imaginations. The casting down begins with the born-again believer. It is not through the flesh that we fight. The fight against the failed-doctrine versions will come through the use of our spiritual weapons. Bring every thought into captivity to the obedience of the Lord Jesus Christ. This is the heart and soul of our Christian life. Led by our Saviour, march on!

Chapter Two
The Panoply–The Whole Armor of God

(Ephesians 6: 13-17) *13 Wherefore take unto you the whole armour of God, that ye may be able to withstand in the evil day, and having done all, to stand. 14 Stand therefore, having your loins girt about with truth, and having on the breastplate of righteousness; 15 And your feet shod with the preparation of the gospel of peace; 16 Above all, taking the shield of faith, wherewith ye shall be able to quench all the fiery darts of the wicked. 17 And take the helmet of salvation, and the sword of the Spirit, which is the word of God:"*

In order for believers to even walk in the Lord, we need to be clothed in the armour that God has given us. The girdle of truth, the breastplate of righteousness, the gospel of peace, the shield of faith, the helmet of salvation, and the sword of the spirit, are the six essentials of this armour.

There is a helmet for our head, the belt, breastplate, a shield, shoes, and a sword. These make a complete set to face the Devil and his minions against all attacks.

We as born-again believers all have the same position in the Lord Jesus Christ. As such, we are all *"blessed with all spiritual blessings in Heavenly places in Christ Jesus"* (Ephesians 1:3b). According to the God's Words in various places, we have been given adoption, wisdom, prudence, forgiveness of sins, understanding, power, and many other blessings.

In the fight against the doctrinal failures in the modern versions, the believer must be armed. There must be preparation for war. We must have our armour on and be in God's power.

Ephesians 6:10 says, *"be strong in the Lord, and in the power of his might."*

If we are living the life of a true Christian as in Ephesians 6, Satan will confront us head on. This is why we need to be *"strong in the Lord."* As we are being offensive and defensive against the Devil's strongholds, he will be attacking right back. The Devil will attack us as individuals and groups in the local church. In the book of Revelation, the Lord Jesus Christ showed us how Satan attacks the church. In Revelation chapters 2 and 3, the letters to the seven churches illustrate the church under attack throughout the age of grace.

What Armour?

> *"Put on the whole armour of God, that ye may be able to stand against the wiles of the devil"* (Ephesians 6:11).
>
> *"...and let us put on the armour of light, ...put ye on the Lord Jesus Christ"* (Romans 13:12b, 14a).

When we have on the armour, we have on the Lord Jesus Christ. We are clothed in Him; we have our protection in Him. When we follow the Lord Jesus Christ we also endure suffering and hardness as good soldiers (2 Timothy 2:3). He is our surrounding and our victory. It is what Christians have on who have gone through unspeakable pain and torture for Jesus and come out victorious.

> *"As it is written, for thy sake we are killed all the day long; we are accounted as sheep for the slaughter. Nay, in all these things we are more than conquerors through him that loved us"* (Romans 8:36-37).

The Girdle of Truth

The belt that a Roman soldier wore tied all the body armour tight to the body. It kept everything close and tight so as to not be grabbed or dragged. It also held the sword. We will cover more on this part of the armour later.

The Breastplate of Righteousness

Every Roman soldier could not do without his breastplate, lest he be hit by an arrow in a vulnerable spot. The righteousness of the Lord Jesus Christ is essential to the believer for without it we cannot see God. The Lord Jesus Christ has redeemed us by His Blood, and for that justification we stand in His righteousness before God. In our battle we need His protection for the bowels, from our neck to our thighs. Our heart is contained therein, containing our emotions and feelings, a prime area of Satanic attacks. This piece makes secure our spiritual and eternal life.

Shoes of the Gospel:

We see the war boots worn by soldiers and they of course protected the feet, and some protected the face of the lower leg, *"...and put the blood of war upon his girdle that was about his loins, and in his shoes that were on his feet."* (1 Kings 2:5b). For the Roman, he wore heavy duty shoes that would take him long distances.

Our shoes of faith must give us a firm foundation, a solid base from which to operate. We need them to be ready to march, just as we need to be prepared with the gospel of peace. We cannot be standing, as it says in Ephesians 6:14 if we are not shod with the faith once delivered. We must be standing in the faith as we engage with the Devil and his wiles. We cannot be slouching or sitting on the sidelines. We are standing our ground in the fierce battle with the Devil. Our power rests in the Lord Jesus Christ. There is no retreat. Our preparation and true walk will give us firmness and solidly bolster our beliefs in Bible doctrines.

The Shield of Faith

Our active faith is a shield that covers the whole body and soul. We have protection promised to us through faith in the Lord Jesus Christ. We have faith that our sins have been blotted out and call God our Father. Our strength through the Lord Jesus Christ can quench any fiery dart of the Devil. All the missiles of the sins of the flesh are hurled our way. To the unregenerate these inflame the passions and incite to physical violence and spiritual chaos. With strong faith, the shield protecting the believer squashes every evil thought passing through the mind and soul. Not given any place in the life of the believer, every dart is deflected away.

The Helmet of Salvation

A most important piece of the armour in the battle would be the helmet. Able to withstand blows to the sensitive head area, so is the hope of the believer when he is assured of such a great salvation. He is covered by the Blood of the Lamb and given great hope as a conqueror for the Lord Jesus Christ. "*Now thanks be unto God, which always causeth us to triumph in Christ,...*" (1 Corinthians 2:14a).

The Sword of the Spirit

This is our main offensive weapon in our battle. The sword of the Spirit is the Words of God, that which we defend, we memorize and wield against the enemy. It is used by the operation of the Holy Spirit through us. This is the only operation which Christians need to be united in the Spirit with. It is sadly much maligned and corrupted and nearly left in shambles by the enemy in the modern church. The Words of God needs to be sharp and ready. We must never be disarmed of it and we must use it continuously.

"For the word of God is quick, and powerful, and sharper than any two edged sword, piercing even to the dividing asunder of soul and spirit, and of the joints and marrow, and is a discerner of the thoughts and intents of the heart" (Hebrews 4:12).

"Therefore judge nothing before the time, until the Lord come, who both will bring to light the hidden things of darkness, and will make manifest the counsels of the hearts; and then shall every man have praise of God" (1 Corinthians 4:5).

So now what? We have all this armour, do we need to wear it? We only need to look to the Apostle Paul to realize the value of our God-given armour. Paul was arrested several times, bitten by a venomous snake, stoned, beaten with rods, five times received thirty-nine stripes, was imprisoned, and many other forms of persecution. He continued to write down the Words of God, preach the gospel, and teach disciples. By his example, we are encouraged to put on the whole armour of God and keep it on and fight the good fight.

"We are troubled on every side, yet not distressed; we are perplexed, but not in despair; persecuted, but not forsaken; cast down, but not destroyed;" (2 Corinthians 4:8-9).

It has to be the Lord who is doing the heavy lifting in this battle. We are only humans, clothed in divinely powered defensive and offensive attire. We are in a spiritual war and we possess spiritual weapons and armour. We have God's call to battle and to take up arms.

"The night is far spent, the day is at hand: let us therefore cast off the works of darkness, and let us put on the armour of light...but put ye on the Lord Jesus Christ,..." (Romans 13: 12, 14a).

Separate yourselves from the chains of sin and be not separated from your God. Darkness does not equate with wearing the armour of light. We cannot put on the Lord Jesus Christ and serve the god of this world. We war against the Devil who is out to destroy all those who would fight for the Lord Jesus Christ. We cannot fight the battles for God's Words without the whole armour of God. Put it on, wear it, don't go anywhere without it.

This is part of God's will for the Christian. He wants us and He commands us to put on and wear the whole armour. He tells us to be "*strong in the Lord.*" Is God being mean, unreasonable, or overbearing? No. It is to be able to withstand the wiles or methods of the Devil. We should not be ignorant of the vile methods of our Adversary. So, we have on the likeness of our Lord and Saviour Jesus Christ in order to withstand and confront our enemy the Devil.

Panoplias, as rendered by the Greek explains that it is the whole armour–the panoply--including every piece, complete, God-given, and empowered by the Holy Spirit. We need it all on, every piece to fight the Lord's battles. There will be no consequences if we keep it all on. This will enable us to stand amidst many foes and be victorious.

It is the wiles of the Devil with which we contend. The Devil will not all of a sudden jump out in front of us and face us squarely. He uses his wiles, *methodeia*, or "methods, devices, and artfulness" against us. He is constantly, methodically, and systematically at work against those pursuing good and God's way.

The Devil is coming out of the darkness to attack. His ways are well planned, skillful, and cunning. Christians should be smart, alert, and more skilled than he is.

> "*That we henceforth be no more children, tossed to and fro, and carried about with every wind of doctrine, by the sleight of men, and cunning*

craftiness, whereby they lie in wait to deceive;" (Ephesians 4:14).

The Devil uses these devices to pull our souls down with him into perdition. He employs deceitful men and women to pull us off the front lines in the battle for the Bible. This cunningness, emerging from the shadows, takes more skill to defeat than something that is directly in the light. The Christian in complete armour is able to meet these attempts to captivate us with darkness and gain the advantage. We employ God's power, standing in His might, to turn back the Devil's covert advances out of the darkness. The enemy will be invisible, we cannot see the Devil. The enemy will be full of deceit as the Devil uses his minions (who are really powerless against the power of God). We need only to be circumspect, expecting a war of ambushes and surprises. This then is our war, one against strategies and wiles.

We cannot be sucked into valleys of pleasure, worldly pursuits, false doctrines, and seeming harmlessness. We do not dare wander so far so that we would be unable to retreat.

> *"But let us, who are of the day, be sober, putting on the breastplate of faith and love; and for an helmet; the hope of salvation"* (1 Thessalonians 5:8).
>
> *"Be sober, be vigilant; because your adversary the devil, as a roaring lion, walketh about, seeking whom he may devour"* (1 Peter 5:8).
>
> *"And the God of peace shall bruise Satan under your feet shortly. The grace of our Lord Jesus Christ be with you. Amen"* (Romans 16:20).

Praying Always

> *"Praying always with all prayer and supplication in the spirit, and watching thereunto with all perseverance and supplication for all saints;"* (Ephesians 6:18).

These are our marching orders. We are outfitted for war. We are spiritual soldiers. We are to pray in order to resist principalities, powers, rulers of darkness in this world, and spiritual wickedness in high places. We are armed. But we are completely dependent upon our commander, the Lord Jesus Christ. As spiritual warriors, we need to be praying with all prayer for all our warfare, our battle plans, and our fellow warriors. It is the spirit of prayer in the Spirit that engages the fight. We should pray without ceasing for the sick, for those in public office, those in business, for our family, while in conferences, and in supplications for the saved and unsaved. We pray anytime and anywhere.

Chapter Three
Truth

"Sanctify them through thy truth: thy word is truth" (John 17:17).

"By the word of truth, by the power of God, by the armour of righteousness on the right hand and on the left, "(2 Corinthians 6:7).

Although this is a defense of the Words of God, and the whole armour discussed, it seems only fitting that the focus should fall upon the truth. The main offensive weapon being the Words of God as embodied in the sword of the Holy Spirit, the belt of truth, having to do with God's truth serves a fundamental purpose for us.

The assumption, therefore, is that the Christian has donned all pieces of the spiritual armour and is in compliance with the Saviour's commands.

"Stand therefore, having your loins girt about with truth," (Ephesians 6:14a).

Stand, having been sanctified and purified.

"For then shalt thou lift up thy face without spot; yea, thou shalt be steadfast, and shalt not fear:" (Job 11:15).

"Ye therefore, beloved, seeing ye know these things before, beware lest ye also, being led away with the error of the wicked, fall from your own steadfastness" (2 Peter 3:17).

The girdle or belt held the garments in place. Moses put upon Aaron a coat and girded that with a belt. Then a robe was put on Aaron along with the ephod and these were belted with the curious girdle of the ephod. The purpose was to have Aaron's garments bound securely to his body (Leviticus 8:7).

Elijah was also girt with a belt of leather about his loins. John the Baptist had his camel's hair clothing secured with a leather girdle (2 Kings 1:8; Mt. 3:4).

In the coming kingdom, *"righteousness"* will be the girdle of the Lord Jesus Christ's loins and *"faithfulness the girdle of His reins"* (Isaiah 11:5).

Our Lord Jesus Christ is pictured in Heaven, by John, as being clothed with a full length garment girt about with a golden girdle. The seven angels with the last plagues are also *"clothed in pure and white linen"* garments and wearing golden girdles (Rev. 1:13; Rev. 15:6).

As being the first piece of armour mentioned, the belt is an important defense of God applied to us Christians. It is part of a whole, meant to withstand the withering attacks of our enemy. The belt plays an important role in the solder's armour. It held the scabbard which in turn held the sword.

The belt of the soldier also held pieces of leather to protect other parts of his body. The belt secured all the other pieces of armour to the body.

This is how the truth of God secures us as we cleave unto the Lord Jesus Christ. Our belt of truth is made up of God's truth, as found in the King James Bible and the underlying Hebrew, Aramaic, and Greek Words. If we do not know or have this truth, how can all other things be held in place?

The church, which is the Lord Jesus Christ's, needs cleansing. This cleansing must replace error with the truth. The errors of the modern Bible versions must be purged and kept clean with God's truth.

> *"Therefore let us keep the feast, not with old leaven, neither with the leaven of malice and wickedness; but with the unleavened bread of sincerity and truth"* (1 Corinthians 5:8).

Here sincerity and truth are used together, almost as syntactical twins. They need not be separated in our understanding of the belt of truth. Adam Clarke makes the connection of the two in Ephesians 6:14, saying, truth may be taken here for "sincerity."

Clarke, in his understanding of this verse (Ephesians 6:14), states that we must know we are clear before God, right in our hearts and intentions, harbor no false beliefs or be hiding sins, or else we are vain in our efforts before God. We must gain confidence and assurance from God. The Words of God gives us this truth and sincerity, it is truth.

This characteristic of God and His Words is elegantly exposited by Pastor J. Paul Reno in an article entitled, "*Sincerity*." He gives this Scripture:

> "*For we are not as many, which corrupt the Word of God: but as of sincerity, but as of God, in the sight of God speak we in Christ*" (2 Corinthians 2:17).

We know that Satan wants to destroy or corrupt the Words of God. He is doing this through the modern versions. He uses the majority of the insincere people to corrupt the Scriptures which we the minority hold dear. The corruption comes when the Words of God are deleted from, added to, or changed in some other way. All the while these corruptions are held out to be still the genuine deal. This is why we need to have our hearts, our minds, and our way of life protected.

When Paul wrote the Words to 2 Corinthians 2:17, the majority were corrupting the truth then! And now today with the new modern versions appearing one every 6 months, the pattern continues. Sincerity in the Greek is the Word, *eilikrineia*, which means "pure, unsullied, free from spot or blemish." Christians that are in the minority are still holding to the cleanness and incorruptibility of God's Words. They are deemed pure in heart and sincere by God.

This squares with the Word, "truth." This Word, "truth," is *aletheia* in the Greek. It is "the unveiled reality lying at the basis of and agreeing with an appearance." It denotes the reality of the truth as revealed before our eyes as opposed to something which is revealed as false or lacking that reality before our eyes.

We know God's Words are truth, they are revealed to us, having read them from the printed page. God tells us His Words are truth.

> "*And ye shall know the truth, and the truth shall make you free*" (John 8:32).

When we read the Bible we want to know that it contains the truth. God tells us it is His truth. The Lord Jesus Christ tells us that He is "*the way, the truth, and the life.*" We can believe and rest in that fact. We can read the King James Bible and know that it is the closest to the truth that man comes to in English. We can rest in that fact and take comfort. However, we cannot read modern versions and rely on them as truth since they fail in so many places the test of truth. This causes us alarm and discomfort.

We cannot depend on the words in modern versions to have the great depth of meaning, (clearness, purity, honesty, without deceit, unadulterated, incorruptible, genuine, undefiled, complete, entire, sound, whole, or true), as we have in the King James Bible.[1] There is that level of understanding of the truth. Our belt of truth reaffirms our trust and sincerity in something that is not corrupt. With this non-corrupt Scripture of the King James Bible, we can use its light to expose the flaws, which turn out to be non-truths in the failed modern versions. We realize the modern versions are not the Words of God at all. They are failed attempts of defiled Bible changes to get money while deceiving the majority of Christians.

So, how very important is it for the soldiers of the Lord Jesus Christ to be belted in truth? Of the utmost. God is truth. God's Words are the truth. The faith once delivered and the practice of the gospel is called the truth. His Bible as truth opposes false teachers and translators.

> *"For the law was given by Moses, but grace and truth came by Jesus Christ"* (John 1:17).
>
> *". . . To this end was I born, and for this cause came I into the world, that I should bear witness unto the truth. Everyone that is of the truth heareth my voice"* (John 18:37b).

This subject is important enough to state a procedure for putting on the belt of truth. Review for some, and first time lesson for others. There is a warfare for the Christian, spiritual in nature against mighty foes which are real in the spirit realm. The Lord Jesus Christ is our strength and our armour, but we are commanded to put on our armour to stand against Satan's methods.

It should be a daily check to see if the armour is securely in place. Especially for a new Christian, prayer must be used for each individual piece of the armour to be put on. To put on is from the Greek, *enduo*, with the idea of "sinking into, to put on as a garment, dress, and clothe oneself." We should be very grateful that our Lord makes provision for our protection. Our minds and hearts need to be kept pure. Besides being in agreement with God about sin, our hearts need to be free from any untruths, bitterness, or malice towards anyone. We need to be sincere in pursuing the truth. Feed on that truth by reading, studying, and delighting in God's Words.

Meditate on those truths learned through the Spirit, storing them in your heart and making them a part of you. Capture every thought and submit it to the truth of God. Walk in the light, which is the Lord Jesus Christ, secure in His strength and power.

> *"And now, O Lord God, thou art that God, thou and thy words be true, and thou hast promised*

this goodness unto thy servant:" (2 Samuel 7:28).

"Set your affection on things above, not on things on the earth. For ye are dead, and your life is hid with Christ in God" (Colossians 3:2, 3).

We will be bombarded daily from keeping our mind on things above. It is like a clam casting off the sand and impurities as it filters through clean water. We allow the truth to enter our minds and hearts, all the while purging the old, useless, selfish thoughts.

Allow the truth to replace the old man's thoughts and allow them to be dead. Feed the new man only and abide in the truth, abide in the Lord Jesus Christ. Do not neglect the truth. Resist worldly, fleshly thoughts and deeds.

". . . It is written, man shall not live by bread alone, but by every word that proceedeth out of the mouth of God" (Matthew 4:4).

"I can do all things through Christ which strengtheneth me" (Philippians 4:13).

Thank the Lord for showing you His truth, for giving us His truth, for showing us that He is the only God. He is our Shepherd, our Wisdom, our Counselor, and our Strength. Thank Him every day.

Now, all this applies to our task at hand. In the battle over versions and their underlying Words, we need to know the truth as God gives us in His Words. His Words are true in the underlying Masoretic and Hebrew and Aramaic and Textus Receptus Greek Words. There is no respect for God's Words today. In denominational schools and churches, incremental drift has occurred in their theology. This has happened step by step in their bibliology. The sound doctrines of inspiration and preservation are being questioned and the authority of Scripture is being removed. The gradual erosion of the beliefs in the

Bible, especially in the use of modern versions of the Bible, have led to a decline in the strength of the church. The attack on our Bible is an attack on our God and on truth. The denominational churches, the charismatic churches, and the emerging churches have not kept rank and have laid the armour aside.

We are not to be conformed to this world. There are Biblical absolutes that need to be adhered to. Turn away from those who would make Bible truths into myths. Keep the belt of truth complete and tight around you. Allow the Spirit of truth to dwell in you and lead you into all truth.

> *"Howbeit when he, the Spirit of truth, is come, He will guide you into all truth..."* (John 16:13a).
>
> *"We are of God: he that knoweth God heareth us; he that is not of God heareth not us. Hereby know we the spirit of truth, and the spirit of error"* (1 John 4:6).

Chapter Four
Our Battleground

The Two Texts

From the time that Almighty God breathed out the Words of the Bible, where did they go from there and what form did they take? The stand taken here is that the Scriptures themselves proclaim that their inspiration, as well as their preservation, are both supernatural.

The Dean Burgon Society from Collingswood, New Jersey, has as its main purpose, the defense of traditional Bible texts. It defends the King James Bible and its underlying Hebrew, Aramaic, and Greek Words.

"The Dean Burgon Society, Inc., proudly takes its name in honor of John William Burgon (1813-1888) the Dean of Chichester in England, whose tireless and accurate scholarship and contribution in the area of New Testament textual criticism; whose defense of the traditional Greek New Testament text against its many enemies; and whose firm belief in the verbal inspiration and inerrancy of the Bible; we believe, have all been unsurpassed either before or since his time!"[1]

It may surprise many Christian's today, and alarm the rest of the majority of uninformed believers, that there are two sets of Hebrew, Aramaic, and Greek Words underlying Bibles today. There's one set that is true, the one that underlies the King James Bible. The other sct of words are corrupt and underlie the modern versions such as the New International Version.

The Bible issue might be new to you. Perhaps you do not understand the need to defend traditional Bible Words or, for that matter, do not possess a copy of a faithful, reliable translation based on such Words.   Sadly, the majority of modern day translations of the world are based on the Westcott and Hort-type of text. The Westcott and Hort Greek text is the foundation of today's Nestle-Aland and the United Bible Societies Greek texts of the New Testament. [2]

Westcott and Hort

These men were two liberal Greek scholars in the Anglican Church of England. Brooke Foss Westcott (1825-1901) and Fenton John Anthony Hort (1828-1892) will be forever remembered in Church history. It was in the year, 1881, that they produced and published their Critical Edition of the Greek New Testament.

Westcott and Hort harbored a deep hatred and resentment for the *"faith once delivered unto the saints"* (Jude 1:3c). Instead they covertly loved and worshipped the apostate Roman Catholic Church and the Virgin Mary.

> *"But the book which has most engaged me is Darwin. ...but at present my feeling is strong that the theory (of evolution) is unanswerable."* [3]
>
> *"No one now, I suppose, holds that the first three chapters of Genesis, for example, give a literal history."* [4]
>
> *"I have been persuaded for many years that Mary-worship and Jesus-Worship have very much in common..."* [5]
>
> *"After leaving the monastery, we shaped our course to a little oratory which we discovered on the summit of a neighboring hill...Fortunately we found the door opened. It is very small, with*

one kneeling place; and behind a screen was a
pieta the size of life (the Virgin Mary with the
dead Christ). ...Had I been alone I could have
knelt there for hours." [6]

These two, Westcott and Hort, were apostates, liberals, and unbelievers. They altered the Greek Words, using the corrupt codex Vaticanus and codex Sinaiticus, giving the world the Westcott-Hort Greek New Testament, which has since gained worldwide acceptance as being the most accurate, authentic, and trustworthy.

Dr. D. A. Waite has written a booklet entitled, *The Theological Heresies of Westcott and Hort* (BFT #595) by which the reader can gain a more thorough understanding.

If we don't understand the part of Westcott and Hort in this, we won't understand why there was the change from the Textus Receptus to the new Westcott-and-Hort type text.[7]

Out of their evil fruit, the WH Greek NT, came a multitude of "evil fruits"–a hundred new English versions and perversions--a corrupt tree cannot bring forth good fruit.[8]

Who was Dean John Burgon?

Most everyone, anywhere, close to the Bible version issue, may ask who is Dean Burgon? They may have heard of Westcott and Hort, but when it comes to Dean John William Burgon (1813-1888) all you hear are crickets. The Dean Burgon Society, recognized by the I.R.S. as a tax exempt organization, takes their name from Dean Burgon, the Dean of Chichester from 1876 to 1888. He was an Anglican cleric in the Chichester Cathedral in Sussex, England. Deans are elected by the four canons, had power delegated to them by the Anglican Bishop, tended to administrative matters, and also had a staff. He fought against apostasy within his own church.

To repeat, Burgon was a man

"whose tireless and accurate scholarship and
contribution in the area of New Testament

*textual criticism; whose defense of the
traditional Greek text against its many enemies;
and whose firm belief in the verbal inspiration
and inerrancy of the Bible, we believe, have all
been unsurpassed either before or since his
time."* [9]

He fought the good fight against any controversial
theological question that arose, and he did it fiercely and
accurately. He was a defender of the Traditional Bible Words
and was against the English Revision. It was known about him
as follows:

*"What a splendid watchdog he is. How loud and
furiously he barks when the smallest danger
threatens the Church or the faith which is
entrusted to the churches keeping. It is the
business of a watchdog to bark furiously and to
even flay at the throat of thieves."* [10]

Today, we have the same Bible battle as Burgon had in his
day. The battle moved from the controversy over the original
Words of the Scripture, to the controversy over the authenticity
of the Scripture, to the controversy over how one interprets or
translates the Scripture.[11]

We find Westcott and Hort, being the liberals that they
were, on the wrong side of every controversy of the time. It was
Westcott and Hort and their theory on New Testament textual
criticism that Dean Burgon met head-on. Burgon gathered
86,489 Church Fathers' (patristic) Scripture quotes. These are
contained in 16 volumes with editing completed by Edward
Miller after his death. These readings were tabulated and found
to be in favor of the Received Text in the gospels, by a majority
of 3 to 2. Here it was believed that the Received or Traditional
Text readings did not exist with the early fathers before 400
B.C. Dean Burgon proved them wrong. They not only existed

before 400 A.D., but made up a plurality of manuscripts, since the corruption was only in a few manuscripts.

Dean Burgon has left us five volumes of work. All have been reprinted by the Dean Burgon Society, Collingswood, New Jersey. The first was *The Last Twelve Verses of Mark.* This book destroys the notion that these last twelve verses do not belong in our King James Bible or are not in the TR. Many, many evidences in the manuscripts are given.

The second book, *The Revision Revised* demolishes the Westcott and Hort false Greek text and theory. The third book by Dean Burgon, reprinted by the DBS, is *The Traditional Text, Volume 1*. This book refutes the false argument that the Greek text did not exist until the Erasmus Greek Text in 1516 A.D. This book provides that the Traditional text was in the possession of the Churches from Apostolic times to the present.

The fourth book, *The Causes of Corruption of the Traditional Text*, Volume II, gives fifteen reasons why the Vatican and Sinai texts corrupted the Traditional text.

The fifth and final book by Dean John Burgon is *Inspiration and Interpretation*. Burgon defends the inerrancy of the Bible in its source language texts, down to the very Words, syllables, and letters. Also, the book has sound principles of Bible interpretation, and an answer to *"Essays and Reviews."*

Dean John William Burgon was a true warrior for Christ in the defense of Traditional texts. We are indebted to his knowledge. We can learn a lot from him as we continue with the banner of Divine truth, standing for the authorized King James Bible and it underlying Hebrew and Greek Words.

The Numbers

What exactly did Westcott and Hort do to the Words of the Greek New Testament?

They

> *"rejected the Textus Receptus in 5,604 places by my actual count. This included 9,970 Greek*

words that were either added, subtracted, or changed from the Textus Receptus. This involves, on the average, 15.4 words per page of the Greek New Testament, or a total of 45.9 pages in all. It is 7% of the total of 140,521 words in the Textus Receptus Greek New Testament." [12]

They were able to get their altered Greek text accepted because F. J. A. Hort, in his *Introduction,* proposed a completely false theory. This *Introduction,* (B.F.T. #1303) persuaded the entire European scholarly world, as well as the United States. B. B. Warfield and the Presbyterians followed Hort. Baptists followed Hort. They managed, with the introduction of their corrupt Greek text, to have the majority of modern Bible scholars adapt the Westcott-Hort text over the Textus Receptus.

Changes in over 5,600 Places

According to D. A. Waite's own counts,

"Using Scrivener's Greek New Testament..., was 5,604 changes that Westcott and Hort made to the Textus Receptus in their own Greek New Testament text. Of these 5,604 alterations, I found 1,952 to be omissions (35%), 467 to be additions (8%) and 3,185 to be changes (57%). In these 5,604 places that were involved in these alterations, there were 4,366 more words included, making a total of 9,970 Greek words that were involved. This means that in a Greek text of 647 pages (such as Scrivener's text), this would average 15.4 words per page that were changed from the Received Text. Pastor Jack Moorman counted 140,521 words in the Textus Receptus. These changes would amount to 7% of the words; and 45.9 pages of the Greek New Testament if placed together in one place." [13]

So, we have all these changes and corruptions done to the false Westcott-Hort Greek texts which number only between 40 and 45 of the written manuscripts extant today. What difference does it make? Isn't it true what people say, the W-H Greek text has omissions, that's true, but they falsely claim that "*no major doctrines are affected?*"

Then they continue:

> "*And if a doctrine or two are taken out here and one there, well it can be found elsewhere in the New Testament.*"

If that's true, and it is taken out of any place, you then have a defective, failed Greek text and a defective, failed English Version based on that failed text.

There's good reason why people are blinded to doctrinal failures in the Westcott-Hort type text. Many writers, many of them good Christian men, some of them apostates, have stated matter-of-factly that doctrine is not affected by the numerous changes in the Westcott-Hort type Greek text or the English modern versions based on them.

We seek to prove them wrong.

Vaticanus "B" and Sinaiticus, Aleph

Five manuscripts dating back to the 4th and 5th centuries give modern scholars that "thrill up their leg." These are referred to as "The five old Uncials." Uncials are large letter hand printed Greek manuscripts. The five are: Aleph, Sinaiticus; A, Alexandrinus; B, Vaticanus; C, Ephraemi Rescriptus; and D, Bezae.

Sinaiticus, written between 350-370 A.D. was discovered by Constantine Tischendorf in 1844 at the monastery of St. Catherine in the foothills of Mt. Sinai. The story goes that he pulled it from a waste basket and rescued it from being used as a fire starter. He then bribed the monks to procure it and later sold it to the Russians, but now it rests in the British Museum. It is probably one of the fifty Bibles requested by Constantine to be made of highest quality paper and vellum (calve skins). Its origin, according to Kenyon, is probably Alexandrian. In just the four gospels 8,872 words are affected in Sinaiticus as compared to the Textus Receptus (Received Text).

Vaticanus B was, as Sinaiticus, written between 350-370 A.D., being one of only two surviving manuscript Bibles that were requested by the Emperor Constantine. Dean Burgon wrote about Vaticanus:

> *"Behold then the altar at which copies, fathers, versions, are all to be ruthlessly sacrificed, the Tribunal from which there shall be absolutely no appeal, - the Oracle which is to silence every doubt, resolve every riddle, smooth away every difficulty. All has been stated, where the name has been pronounced of – Codex B."* [14]

It bounced around the world for over 1,100 years and ended up in the Vatican library. The reason that B and Aleph have survived, in relatively good shape for their age, is that they were never used by Christians. Its text associates itself along with Aleph and Alexandria. A total of 7,578 words have been somehow altered in B as compared to the TR according to Burgon.

For all their alterations and corruptions, B and Aleph are the two pillars on which Westcott and Hort built their Greek New Testament text designed to dethrone the TR.

Westcott and Hort New Testament Greek

Westcott and Hort put together a New Testament Greek text. They started it in the 1850's, and provided it for the Revised Version Committee which completed their work in 1881 on the English Revised Version (ERV). This text relied mostly on the Vatican B Gnostic manuscript and Sinaiticus. With the Greek text, and Hort's *Introduction to the Greek New Testament*, scholars at that time were influenced to switch form the Received Text to the Westcott and Hort Greek text. First, there was the English Revised Version (ERV), and next the American Standard Version (ASV). They were both said to be better because they were based on the Westcott and Hort Greek text.

Nestle-Aland (NA) and UBS (4th edition) Greek Texts

After the Westcott and Hort Greek text, came Eberhard Nestle who edited the Greek text which Kurt Aland later worked on. The NA text reached its 25th edition in 1963, and is currently in its 28th edition (NA28).

In 1955, another Greek text was started by the United Bible Societies. This committee was headed up by apostates Eugene Nida, Bruce Metzger, and also included Kurt Aland. Allen Wikgren of Chicago, Illinois, also helped. In 1966, Roman Catholic Jesuit Cardinal Carlo Maria Martini, rector of the Pontifical Biblical Institute of Rome, was added.

In the preface of the 1st edition in 1966, it was stated that the work on this Greek text was carried out "on the basis of Westcott and Hort's edition."[15] The second edition appeared two years hence. With the publication of UBS/3 in 1975, and Nestle Aland 26 in 1979, the quest for textual identity between the two editions was realized.[16]

This is the "Critical Text" (CT). The Nestle-Aland text serves as the basis for most modern Bible versions. It is also the "standard" in the Greek Departments in seminaries and liberal learning Bible colleges. UBS/4 has found use for foreign translators and missionaries. It must be emphasized that these texts that theological liberals and apostates put together was done in rejection of the Traditional Bible Words that underlie our King James Bible.

Received Text (TR)

The King James Bible is the translation of the Hebrew Masoretic text, and the Greek New Testament text known as the

Textus Receptus. This was the text that was used and accepted by the Churches since apostolic times (see appendix B). In over 5,440 manuscripts today, approximately 99% are represented by the Textus Receptus, while 1% make up the Critical Text.

The first printed Greek Received text, was in 1516, by Erasmus. In 1522, Erasmus printed his 3rd edition of the Greek New Testament. Stephanus published Greek NT texts from 1546 to 1551. The Beza's Greek Textus Receptus was printed in 1598. Beza's text was basically the Greek NT text that the King James Bible was based on. The 1624 Greek text, published by the Elziver Brothers, was also a Received Text.

The Received Text, Textus Receptus, has survived the test of time for us, from the time of the apostles until now. The Words of the Received Greek and Masoretic Hebrew and Aramaic texts that underlie the King James Bible are the very Words which God has preserved down through the centuries, being the exact Words of the original Autographs themselves.[17]

Chapter Five
Inspiration

Objectives Of The Dean Burgon Society

"*3. To defend the Traditional Masoretic Hebrew Text of the Old Testament which underlies the King James version.*"

"*4. To defend the Traditional Greek Text of the New Testament which underlies the King James Version (such as is found in The Greek Text Underlying The English Authorized Version of 1611).*"

"*5. To defend the Traditional Translation of the Bible--the King James Version (or Authorized Version) as a true, faithful, and accurate translation from the underlying original Texts which have been providentially preserved for us, which Translation has no equal in our time among all of the other English 'Translations'.*"

"*6. To expose and publicize the defects, deficiencies, errors, and mistakes both in the texts used and in the translation process and results of any and all modern translations of the Bible, whether in English, or in other languages, which are NOT based on the Traditional Masoretic Hebrew Text and Traditional Received Greek Text which underlie the King James Version.*" [1]

Perhaps the biggest failure within the church today does not even involve a modern Bible perversion.

The total misunderstanding and misuse of the term and doctrine of inspiration is leading Christians to say that a translation such as the King James Bible is inspired. There is nothing farther from the truth, as we shall see.

> *"All scripture is given by inspiration of God, and is profitable for doctrine, for reproof, for correction, for instruction in righteousness:"* (II Timothy 3:16)

> *"For the prophesy came not in old time by the will of man: but holy men of God spake as they were moved by the Holy Ghost."* (II Peter 1:21)

This is the battle that rages today: Is the King James Bible inspired? It seems such an innocuous question. Can the English language King James Bible be held up and claimed to be *"given by inspiration of God?"* Can we say that the King James Bible is *"inspired of God?"* Is it *"verbally inspired?"* Does it possess *"derivative inspiration?"* How about *"indirect inspiration,"* *"having the mark of inspiration,"* or *"inspired in a 'generic' sense?"*

To hold up and call the King James Bible the inspired Words of God, as many have done, is unbiblical. But just the opposite is said today, and anyone who disagrees is shouted down, verbally abused, and called terrible names. This is exactly the point of attack being used by the Devil at this very moment to destroy the Words of God and the faith of millions of Christians.

Satan's top general leading the attack on our King James Bible is Dr. Peter S. Ruckman of Pensacola, Florida. Dr. R.L. Hymers describes Ruckmanism this way:

> *"Ruckmanism is the belief that the KJV translation is given by inspiration of God; the translation itself is preserved, and the*

translation is superior to and corrects the Greek and Hebrew Bible from which it was translated."[2]

If you ask Baptist leaders if they hold to any of Ruckmanism's tenets, they most likely will refuse to answer you. If they do answer, they will deny being a Ruckmanite, as does Ruckman himself.

The first tenet of Ruckmanism, upon which all the others rest, is the belief that the King James Version was "*given by inspiration of God.*"[3] He does not say that the King James Bible is "*inspired*" but "*given by inspiration of God.*" These two points are interchangeable. Of course Ruckman refers to "*all scripture*" in II Timothy 3:16 as being every copy of the Scriptures ever made and not the original autographs.

But Ruckman considers any copies with errors in them as not being Scripture. Only the accurate copies of the originals can be called Scripture, and those are the ones given by inspiration, or "*inspired*". II Timothy 3:16 says nothing about copies being given by inspiration, but proven only by the twisted logic of Peter S. Ruckman. His logic:

1. Major premise: "*The King James Bible says, 'all scripture is given by inspiration of God'*" (2 Tim. 3:16).

2. Minor premise: "*The verse I just quoted was scripture*" (2 Tim. 3:16).

3. Conclusion: "*The King James Bible was 'given by inspiration of God'*" (2 Timothy 3:16)

The point is that you cannot assume your conclusion in advance, and build the major and minor premises from that. One logically draws a conclusion from the major and minor premises.

How can we define the very technical term God uses in Scripture to give us His Words?

Inspiration

Dr. D.A. Waite, Th.D., PhD, President of the Dean Burgon Society has defined the Greek Word for inspiration. We can quote the Verse, II Timothy 3:16a, *"all scripture is given by inspiration of God..."*

The five English words in the King James, *"given by inspiration of God,"* are a proper translation of one Greek Word. That Greek Word is *"theopneustos."* This is a compound word made up of the two other Greek Words. *"Theo"* is short for *"theos"* which means God. *"Pneustos"* is an adjective from the verb, *"pneo"* which means *"to breathe."* The literal meaning of this Greek Word, *"theopneustos"* is *"God-breathed."* So, inspiration is a process by which God breathed out His Words from Genesis to Revelation. That process stopped with the last Words of Revelation, closing the Canon.

What is it that is *"given by inspiration of God"*?

a) It is *"all scripture"*

b) this is *"Pasa"* (all) and *"graphe"* (Scripture). *"graphe"* refers to that which is "written down". [5]

What was "written down"?

God spoke in Hebrew, Aramaic, and Greek Words.

a) God "breathed out" these Words in Hebrew, Aramaic, and Greek.

So, strictly speaking, the only Words that were "breathed out" or "inspired Words" were the Hebrew, Aramaic, and Greek Words God gave to the writers. [6]

So, where does anybody get the idea that inspiration could refer to translations? God did not *"breathe out"* and does not *"breathe out"* English, French, Chinese, Russian, Italian, Japanese, or Bantu words. Frankly speaking, words translated in Bible translations are not "breathed out" or "inspired," but "translated" words.

The Bible (be persuaded), in the Hebrew, Aramaic, and Greek, is the very utterance of the eternal; as much God's

Words, as if high Heaven were open, and we heard God speaking to us with human voice. Every book of it, is inspired alike; and is inspired entirely. The apocryphal books are not one atom more inspired than Bacon's essays. But the Bible, from the alpha to the omega of it, is filled to overflowing with the Holy Spirit of God: the books of it and the sentences of it, and the Words of it and the syllables of it, aye, and the very letters of it.[7]

Dr. Thomas M. Strouse, of Emmanuel Baptist Seminary, has written an essay, *"The Translation Model Predicted by Scripture."* He states, the Bible attests to its own inspiration. Inspiration is the process whereby the Holy Spirit led the writers of Scripture to record accurately His very Words; the product of this process was the inspired originals. In II Timothy 3:16 are key Words and their respective syntax. The key Words for proper bibliological understanding are "all" (pasa), "Scripture" (graphe), and *"is given by inspiration of God"* (theopneustos). *"Pasa"* may be translated as "all" when used with technical nouns. When *"pasa"* is used with an anarthros noun that is technical, it should be translated as "all".

The expression *"all scripture"* declares the inspiration of all the Words of the Bible. The Word *"graphe"* is a technical noun in the Bible for *"scripture."* John 5:39; Acts 17:2; Romans 1:2; and II Peter 1:20; are examples of Biblical writers using the Words *"graphe"* to refer to the whole collection of the books of the Bible.

The Word *"theopneustos"* Strouse continues, is translated with six words in the King James Bible, including the verb: *"is given by inspiration of God"* since *"theopneustos"* is a verbal adjective and has a passive sense, grammatically it may be translated as the King James rendering *"is given by inspiration of God."*

Deciding where to place the "is" affects the meaning of the verse. If *"theopneustos"* is translated as an attributive adjective, then the "is" would come after "*theopneustos*" and be rendered "*every God inspired Scripture is profitable,*" suggesting that some Scripture might not be inspired. If "*theopneustos*" is translated as a predicate adjective then the "is" would be placed before "*theopneustos*" and rendered "*all scripture is God inspired and is profitable.*" Since "*graphe*" is a technical term and therefore treated as a definite noun, the Greek construction adjective ("*pasa*") plus noun ("*graphe*") plus adjective ("*theopneustos*") must be understood as predicate, placing the "is" prior to the second adjective.

Paul's technical expression of inspiration demands a technical translation and application of "*theopneustos.*" All the original autographs (from Genesis to Revelation) were inspired, but only the original autographs were inspired. "*Inspired*" may not be applied to the original writers, the non-Canonical words of the Lord Jesus Christ or the apostles, to any Hebrew or Greek manuscripts, or to any Bible translations. The King James Bible rendering of this verse is both accurate and specific. The Bible self-attests to verbal, plenary, inspiration of the autographs.[8]

The proper interpretation of II Timothy 3:16 is that it refers solely to the Hebrew, Aramaic, and Greek Words that were originally given by God. The wrong interpretation of this verse is that it flat out refers to the King James Bible or any other translation.

Those who speak of an inspired King James Bible fail to take into account some glaring facts. Such as, which edition of the King James Bible contains the God-breathed Words? Do they mean any of the special editions of the King James Bible that came out in: 1613, 1616, 1617, 1618, 1629, 1630, 1633, 1634, 1637, 1638, 1640, 1642, 1653, 1659, 1675, 1679, 1833, 1896, or 1904? How about two of the "curious" editions that came out in; 1611, the Great "He" Bible, (Ruth 3:15, "and he went into the city.") or, the 1611, "Judas" Bible, (Matthew 26:36, "Judas" for "Jesus").

Also, it is impossible for our perfect God to "breathe-out" the Apocrypha. The translators wrongly included it in the 1611 KJB, but it was removed a few short years after.

It could be noted that eastern orthodoxy still maintained that the Apocrypha was not only a part of their Bible, but they believed it was sacred Scripture. [9]

King James Bible--Translated not "Inspired"

"But I do not believe, as many who use it and stand in favor of it, that the KJB is either "inspired," "given by inspiration of God," "inspired by God," or "God-breathed." Neither do I believe, as many who use it and stand in favor of it, that the KJB is referred to in Psalm 12:6-7. These verses refer to the Hebrew and Aramaic Old Testament (and, by extension to the New Testament Greek) words where God has promised to preserve them. English was not even in existence at the time when Psalm 12:6-7 was written, nor was any other modern language then in existence. It is incorrect to assume that Psalm 12:6-7 refers to the KJB translation. Peter Ruckman, Gail Riplinger and their followers, and many others believe and teach this. I believe this is a serious doctrinal error regarding the King James Bible."[10]

We must reiterate that the New Testament teaches what the meaning of inspiration is. The King James Bible translates the Greek Word, *"theopneustos,"* to mean *"God-breathed,"* or *"breathed out by God."* One can never consider any translation in any of the world's languages, to mean *"breathed out by God."*

In every translation, no matter in what language you are referring to, you have the work of translators interpreting that language what God Himself has *"inspired"* or *"breathed out"* in

His original Hebrew, Aramaic, or Greek Words. God *"breathed out"* or *"inspired"* only His original Hebrew, Aramaic, and Greek Words. [11]

As regards to the Dean Burgon Society (DBS), an organization that defends the King James Bible and its underlying Words, this statement about the Bible is from the articles of faith (1978):

A. The Bible

"We believe in the plenary, verbal, divine inspiration of the sixty-six canonical books of the Old and the New Testaments (from Genesis to Revelation) in the original languages, and in their consequent infallibility and inerrancy in all matters of which they speak (2 Timothy 3:16-17; 2 Peter 1:21; 1 Thessalonians 2:13). The books known as the Apocrypha, however, are not the inspired word of God in any sense whatsoever. As the Bible uses the term "inspiration" it refers to the writings, not the writers (2 Timothy 3:16-17); the writers are spoken of as being "holy men of God" who were "moved," "carried" or borne" along by the Holy Spirit (2 Peter 1:21) in such a definite way that their writings were supernaturally, plenarily, and verbally inspired, free from any error, infallible, and inerrant, as no other writings have ever been or ever will be inspired.

We believe that the King James Bible Version (or Authorized Version) of the English Bible is a true, faithful, and accurate translation of these two providentially preserved texts, which in our time has no equal among all of the other English translations. The translators did such a fine job in their translation task, that we can without apology hold up the Authorized Version of 1611 and say "this is the word of God."

We believe that all the verses in the King James Version belong in the Old and the New Testaments because they represent words we believe were in the original texts..."[12]

No "Inspired" King James Bible

The DBS back in 2002 settled the issue of an inspired translation amongst its leaders.

Reaffirming that over the previous 25 years before 2002, its articles of faith had never stated or believed that the King James Bible or any translation was "inspired." There had been confusion on this subject within the DBS and throughout the Christian world. Therefore, the leaders of the Dean Burgon Society overwhelmingly agreed to clarify this issue. The articles of faith limit "inspiration," "inspired," or "God-breathed" to the Words of the Old Testament Hebrew or Aramaic and the New Testament Words of Greek. They agreed that there is no reference to any translation, whether in English, French, German, Italian, or in any other language be either *"inspired," "given by inspiration of God,"* or God-breathed." All DBS leaders are united in the position that 2 Timothy 3:16, the central verse for things that are *"inspired by God," "given by inspiration of God,"* and *"God-breathed"* do not refer to translations, no matter how accurate they are.

In fact it goes further. The words of translations were not breathed-out by God in any of the various translations of the world. God did not do that. Men translated them. For anyone to state that God "breathed-out" the translations of the world would be by definition affirming *"double inspiration by God."* This doctrine, falsely acclaimed, must be rejected by all Bible-believing Christians. There is still much confusion about what is meant by the words *"given by inspiration of God"* (2 Timothy

3:16). It behooves every redeemed believer to clearly understand the terms properly. Many have learned this incorrectly and now they must unlearn the error.

To stem any further confusion and to be clear for the future the DBS has modified its yearly questionnaire/application to reflect DBS articles on the Bible. Specifically, question #2 reads:

"2. [   ] I agree, [   ] I cannot agree – to follow unequivocally our DBS official position referring to the King James Bible as stated in our DBS articles and other documents.

a. Because I believe it to be the correct and proper Biblical position, I will reserve the following five terms exclusively for the Hebrew, Aramaic, and Greek Words underlying the King James Bible: "given by inspiration of God," "God-breathed," "inspired of God," "verbally inspired," or "inspired" [see note at the end of this paragraph] (2 Timothy 3:16). [DBS Articles, p. 3, Bible Preservation, p. 7 "K"] I will not use any of these preceding five terms to anyone, at any time, in anyway, at anyplace to refer to the words of the King James Bible or any other translation, because I am in full agreement that to do so is not Biblical. I believe this position is consistent with our DBS articles and other DBS documents.

[Note: Neither the King James Bible or any other language translation, will be referred to as "inspired" in any sense at all, including "derivative inspiration," "indirect inspiration," "having the mark of inspiration," "inspired in a 'generic' or general sense" or any other similar

terms that might be brought up to modify "inspired" or "inspiration."] [13]

Derivative Inspiration

An inspired translation belief can also lead to other fallacies, such as derivative inspiration. Derivative inspiration is a belief that translated Bible's Words derive inspiration from the underlying original Words. This position rejects the God-breathed definition of inspiration, (theopneustos). This belief also confuses the Bible's claim that inspiration was just "once delivered" (Jude 1:3) by de-emphasizing once given thus confusing the issue.

Double-Inspiration

Mentioned before, the need is to double down on this definition. Double inspiration simply means that God breathed out the words of a translation, such as the King James Bible. Scripture shows us that the inspired Words were only given once by God.

Theories of Biblical Inspiration

Plenary Inspiration: The full Bible is inspired, every bit of it, all of the Words of God are breathed-out.

Verbal Inspiration: The writing of the Bible is of the living God. Each letter, each Word, each sentence was given by the Holy Spirit.

False Views of Inspiration

Natural Inspiration: Says that the Scriptures are the product of intelligent men. These so-called gifted or intelligent men put to writing such an excellent spiritual literature that it would just appear to be inspired. It is a modernist idea that teaches man can develop inspiration naturally on his own. Surely this is folly since it would derive from sinful man.

Partial Inspiration: Says that only certain parts of the Bible are inspired and others are not. It teaches that the Bible merely contains the Words of God. [14]

Partial theory gives man the authority to decide which parts of Scripture are inspired and which are not. Therefore, a man can say the Bible speaks with authority in morality and doctrine, but is not authoritative in science, geography or history. This makes this theory to be deeply subjective and is not what the Bible says about itself. (2 Timothy 3:16).

Conceptual Inspiration

This unscriptural idea says that God only inspired the thoughts of the Bible and man wrote those thoughts down in his own words.[15]

This conception of inspiration is pure nonsense. If God did not breathe-out His Words then we cannot be sure the thoughts written down were from God. It appeared that some of the writers did not even understand what they were writing. (Daniel 7:15-16; 12:8-9). God had to say every Word so that it could be written down.

Inspired King James Bible?

A prime example of a dear Pastor, now departed and knowing better, who did not have a clear understanding of inspiration was Perry F. Rockwood (1917-2008).

An article was reprinted by Pastor Rockwood and appeared in the Gospel Standard in the May, 2011 issue. The Gospel Standard is published by the Peoples Gospel Hour, Halifax, Nova Scotia, of which Pastor Rockwood was the founding editor. His title says it all about this battle; "*The Inspired King James Bible,*" He stated; "*If scripture is inspired, and all scripture is inspired of God.*" This sounds good, but we know that we must be more precise in these apostate times. The word inspired has been hijacked and we need to retrieve it back. The word inspired has been already defined. The Scripture was given in Hebrew, Aramaic, and Greek by God. This needs to be mentioned again and again until it is universally understood.

Pastor Rockwood then attacks without any provocation *"The following statement by D. A. Waite and the Dean Burgon Society is wrong"*:

> *"There is no reference whatsoever that any translation, whether in English, French, German, Italian, or any other language, should be termed either 'inspired,' 'given by inspiration of God,' or 'God-breathed' (all meaning the same thing)."*[16]

Hopefully, we have all begun learning that translations are not *"inspired."* But, as proof would have it, it turns out that there is much work left to be done. The situation is beyond urgent; it is life-support or die. Witness a question and answer posed on the *"Ruckman Exposed"* Facebook site on March 31, 2013.

Question: Do you know if Peter Ruckman believes in multiple inspired Bible translations like he does the KJB?

A self-proclaimed follower of Peter Ruckman answers:

> *"The easiest way I can explain something spiritually discerned like that to a spiritual babe, or to a lost person who cannot comprehend spiritual matters, and who will follow LOST MEN* (emphasis Jesse Sargent) *in "translating" Catholic manuscripts to compete with the King James Bible; is that the Bible says, all scripture is given by inspiration. Therefore, if I quote some scripture to you, as I just did, it is inspired even when I quote it. If you will then, you may call it INFINITE* (emphasis his) *inspiration of scripture, BIBLICALLY* (emphasis his) *speaking, unless you are a Biblical illiterate."* (Jesse Sargent)

Chapter Six
Preservation

The Issue

The doctrine of verbal, plenary inspiration of the Bible and divine preservation of the Bible go hand in hand together. We declare that God breathed-out the Words which are His Words in Hebrew, Aramaic, and Greek. God then preserved those Hebrew, Aramaic, and Greek Words through time to the present.

Textual Critics

Modern day Textual Critics base their arguments and opposition on assumptions that the Bible is like any ordinary book. Nothing supernatural happened to land us any of God's Words. God did no revealing of Himself through divine Words. No, we need to look beyond words to a mere message giving God to men who put that message in their own words. That makes the Bible a human book and that is the direction from which comes the attack on believers in a divinely Worded Bible. Were God's thoughts in human words the only things given to us? We believe that the breathed-out Words making up the Bible in their entirety were given to us by God. If they are only man's words then they are subject to corruption as is any other written material. This opens the door to Modern Textual Criticism and its methods, in hopes of restoring the Bible back to what we already have been given to us by God.

Daniel Wallace, a constant critic of the Textus Receptus, has said,

*"In sum, a theological a priori has no
place in textual criticism. Since this is the
case, it is necessary to lay aside fideism
in dealing with the evidence."* [1]

Wallace joins the chorus of New Testament textual critics in
pronouncing the Textus Receptus dead. Wallace quotes many
apostates to add to his approval:

*"A. T. Robertson, in 1926, declared, "The Textus
Receptus is as dead as Queen Anne." Eight
years later Leo Vaganay similarly pronounced
last rites over the corpse. And just three decades
ago, in his text of the New Testament, Bruce
Metzger could justifiably dismiss the
contemporary defense of the Byzantine text in a
mere footnote."* [2]

The Real Issue

Such high and mighty, nose-bleed company, for sure. But
what is the real issue here? There must be something more, to
so eagerly sweep aside the matchless documents and over 5,000
manuscripts called the TR.

*"There is an agenda in theological circles.
American Evangelical theologians are seeking
the approval of apostate theologians of Europe.
(I call them the dead Germans Society.) To do so
they have had to mature. Part of that process is
getting past the provincial fundamentalist belief
that the Bible is the authoritative, verbally
inspired, divinely preserved word of God. They
have worked out a formula which allows them to
satisfy the Dead Germans Society and still pay
lip service to traditional evangelical doctrinal
statements on the inspiration and preservation of
the Scriptures. But, there is one problem. As long
as there is a legitimate, academic defense of the*

> *King James Bible and the texts from which it*
> *comes, their position is exposed for what it is,*
> *compromise. Therefore, they want to destroy the*
> *credibility of anyone who would attempt to*
> *academically defend the King James Bible and*
> *the texts from which it come, that is, us. We are*
> *an embarrassment to them..."*[3]

God inspired the Words of Scripture and preserved them to
today.

> *"The situation today is disturbingly*
> *different. Gone is the era when KJV/TR*
> *advocates could be found only in the*
> *backwaters of anti-intellectual American*
> *fundamentalism. A small but growing*
> *number of students of the NT in North*
> *America and, to a lesser degree, in*
> *Europe (in particular the Netherlands*
> *and Great Britain) are embracing a view*
> *that was left for dead more than a*
> *century ago – namely, that the original*
> *text is to be found in a majority of MSS*
> *(manuscripts)."*[4]

It cannot be stated enough, as long as there are edited,
emended texts, such as the Nestle-Aland and United Bible
Societies Critical Texts, they will be vehicles for the infusion of
the wisdom of men into the Words of God. These malleable
texts can be made to fit any theological view and as such are
much more desirable.

The Textual scholar works from the platform that the Bible
never had any providential protection preserving it. If these
critics accept God as the Bible's source, the actual Words of
God can only be restored to some near approximation of the
originals. In their minds the Bible is all about God, His
message, ideas and thoughts, but it is not the Words of God. We

must experience the Words for them to be the Words of God. The preserved and correct text is not important to these Modern Critics. The closest and most accurate translation, our King James Bible, is not important to them.

Our faith, that we have the Words of God preserved in the Hebrew, Aramaic, and Greek, and most accurately translated in the King James Bible gives us our conviction. Our belief leaves no room for twisting the Scriptures and inventing strange doctrines. We mature in God's Words and seek to please no dead–soul Europeans. Scriptures that teach the doctrine of preservation will be used and understood to mean that the Bible is the Word of God.

> *"In questions relating to the inspired word, mere speculation and unreason have no place. In short, the Traditional Text, founded upon the vast majority of authorities and upon the rock of Christ's church, will, if I mistake not, be found upon examination to be out of all comparison superior to a text of the nineteenth century, whatever skill and ingenuity may have been expended upon the production or the defense of it."*[5]
>
> *"...For as concerning this sect, we know that everywhere it is spoken against."* (Acts 28:22b)
>
> *"For the heart of this people is waxed gross, and their ears are dull of hearing, and their eyes have they closed; lest they should see with their eyes, and hear with their ears, and understand with their heart, and should be converted, and I should heal them."* (Acts 28:27)
>
> *"Perverse disputings of men of corrupt minds, and destitute of the truth, supposing that gain is godliness: from such withdraw thyself."* (1 Timothy 6:5)

It is Written

To understand Bible preservation we need to understand what the Lord Jesus Christ said about it. When Jesus was tempted by the Devil's three tests, the Lord Jesus Christ answered three times beginning with the Words, *"It is written."* That referred to the Old Testament in Deuteronomy 8:3; 6:16; 6:13 and 10:20.

First of all, in regards to Matthew 4:4, how can we live by every Word of God unless His Words have been preserved for us? We may not know Hebrew or Greek so we must have it accurately translated into English. By quoting form the Old Testament, and more accurately, from Deuteronomy, our Lord is telling us all that the Words in Hebrew in the Old Testament have been preserved up to our present day.

We should look at the Words: *"It is written."* This is the perfect tense in Greek and must be understood if we have any chance of understanding Bible preservation. "It" is *gegraptai.* The root verb means "to write." Our English word, "graphite" comes from this word, as well as the word, "mimeograph." Grapho is the Greek Word for "write" and *gegraptai* is the perfect tense of that verb. There are three main tenses in Greek. 1) There is the imperfect past tense, which is the progressive past "was writing." 2) There is the aorist past, which is a spot or point action, "wrote." 3) Then you have another past tense, the perfect tense which is used here.

According to "the intermediate grammar of the Greek New Testament," by Dana and Mantey, pages 200-205, the perfect tense indicates an action has begun in the past and the results of that act continue right on down to the very present."[6]

God Promised the Preservation of His Words

Every time the Word *gegraptai* is used in the perfect tense of that verb, we have proof of God's preservation of the Bible. It is preserved in the Hebrew and Greek, and faithfully and accurately translated for us in the King James Bible.

Besides the proof that the Hebrew and Greek Words are preserved, we have proof that God promised to preserve all those Words.

> *"If the foundations be destroyed,*
> *what can the righteous do?"*
> (Psalm 11:3)

Our foundation is the Bible. All of God's doctrines come from God's book, the Bible. The right English Bible wherein is found all doctrine, is the King James Bible. God's Words secure His promises to preserve His Words.

> *"God is not a man that he should lie; neither the*
> *son of man, that he should repent: hath he said,*
> *and shall he not do it? Or hath he spoken, and*
> *shall he not make it good?"* (Numbers 23:19)

God is not a man capable of lying as men are. We can put our full trust in Him to do what He says He will do.

> *"The words of the Lord are pure words: as*
> *silver tried in a furnace of earth, purified seven*
> *times. 7 Thou shalt keep them, O Lord, thou shalt*
> *preserve them from this generation for ever."*
> (Psalm 12:6, 7) (Psalm 78:1-7)

"Thou shalt keep them," and *"thou shalt preserve them,"* (Psalm 12:7), are contentiously held by the Modern Textual Critics today, to mean the righteous rather than the Words are preserved. Reading verses 3 to 5, the Lord has already promised to protect the righteous and keep him safe. The antecedent, or a substantive word, phrase, or clause referred to by a pronoun, is the last grammatically matching noun. The pronoun in verse 7 is the plural, them. The antecedent nouns that are plural are the Words, and the wicked. Since we know that God does not promise to preserve the wicked, there can only be one conclusion and that would be that God preserves the Words of the Lord. It would also violate the laws of grammar to say God would preserve the righteous man which is in the singular.

As is usually pointed out there is a gender discordance and this can be properly interpreted.

> ". . . *the pronominal suffix "Keep them" in verse 7a is in the masculine gender (plural). "The words of the Lord" in verse 6 is in the feminine gender (plural). "them" must refer to "people". In order for it to refer to God's word the pronominal suffix must also be in the feminine gender like the substantive. This is a faulty reasoning based upon a wrong assumption. As Gesenius, a classic Hebrew grammarian teaches, 'through a weakening in the distinction of gender, which is noticeable elsewhere. And which probably passed from the colloquial language into that of literature, masculine suffixes (especially in the plural) are not infrequently used to refer to feminine substantives'!" [Gesenius' Hebrew Grammar, edited and enlarged by E. Kitsch, 2nd ed. By N. E. Crowley, CT, P440, Sec.O.]* [7]

There are examples in the Old Testament where we find masculine plural suffixes referring to feminine substantives; Genesis 31:9, 32:15; Exodus 1:21; Psalm 119:111; 129, 152, 167. Therefore, according to Hebrew grammar it is perfectly right to refer the suffix pronoun, "them (masculine plural, verse 7a), to "the Words" (feminine plural, verse 6) of the Lord in Psalm 12:6,7. This is then an example of God's divine preservation.

False Ideas on Preservation

Raymond Blanton has given us four types of preservation that are false and attack God and His Words. Again, we believe, as Christians, that God has breathed out (inspired) Hebrew, Aramaic, and Greek Words that are found today in the

Masoretic Texts, and the Greek Textus Receptus. Some false notions on preservation include:

1.   Fragmented Preservation: We are told by liberal theologians that there are lost books of the Bible that should be considered as Canon. There are no lost books of the Bible! We can be assured that there are 66 Canonical books that make up the Bible. All of the Words of the Bible are preserved and none are lost, even though modern day textual critics may think and say so.

2. Remote Preservation: It is true that God's Words are settled in Heaven. But God chose to reveal those Words to us on earth and preserve those Words for us. His Words are not buried somewhere, but are in the possession of God's children at all times.

"But the word is very nigh unto thee..." (Deuteronomy 30:14)

"Thy word have I hid in mine heart..." (Psalm 119:11)

3. Mingled Preservation: This is the type where self-righteous preachers interject their better renderings upon what the Scriptures say. You cannot have preserved Words, faithfully translated, if you are mingling man's words and interpretations with them. The ideal is to sow the good seed in good soil. Faith comes by hearing the correct Words of God and not man's idea about what those Words are or mean. We are not saved by corruptible seed but by incorruptible seed.

> *"Being born again, not of corruptible seed, but of incorruptible, by the word of God, which liveth and abideth for ever."* (1 Peter 1:23)

4. Reasonable Facsimile Preservation: This is probably the most prevalent error of our day. God has preserved His Words, in the Masoretic Texts and the Textus Receptus, not simply His thoughts, ideas, message, concepts, truth, or teachings. It's His original Words that are preserved. This perverts the true idea of God's preservation, the doctrine of the inerrancy of God's preservation, the doctrine of the inerrancy of the preserved Scriptures. This leads to the attack that no major doctrines are affected by the corrupt perversions of the Modern Versions. These modern critics are quoting Philip Mauro with approval:

> *"That the sum of all the variant readings taken together does not give ground for the slightest doubt as to any of the fundamental points of faith and doctrine."*

This is flatly false. One only needs to check out Dr. Jack Moorman's book: *Three Hundred Fifty-Six Doctrinal Errors in the N.I.V. and Other Modern Bible Versions.*

Further Mayhem: Fundamentalist Deception on Bible Preservation

Modern writers have been warned about false beliefs in reasonable facsimile preservation. Dr. D. A. Waite has written 3 books about this, regarding staff members of Bob Jones University and writers connected to that university. They are: *Bob Jones University's Errors on Bible Preservation*; *Fundamentalist Misinformation on Bible Versions*; and *Fundamentalist Deception on Bible Preservation.*

From the Mind of God to the Mind of Man was a book published in August, 1999. It had very helpful support from Dr. Bob Jones III, president of Bob Jones University. It was written by graduates, faculty members, trustee board members, cooperating board members, and friends of Bob Jones University. What is sad about the information in this book is that it is misinformation from those who call themselves fundamentalists. This has the effect of perversely influencing Bible institutes, colleges, universities, churches, and individuals both in the United States and on many of the mission fields of the world.

Some of the misinformation contained in this book includes;
"The BJU Committee offered for example that Bible preservation of the words of Hebrew and Greek was information not based in either Scripture or historical fact."[8]
Another example of misinformation from BJU is found on page 16 of *The Mind of Man*. Dr. Shaylor wrote:
"The Preservation of Revelation–God has made His revelation available to others than those to whom it was immediately given by preserving His truth in written form."[9]
Dr. Shaylor is writing about the *"Preservation of Revelation,"* but he nowhere says God has preserved His Words. He just says it's simply His truth. This is not Biblical preservation unless the Words are preserved. [10]
The next book that Dr. Waite wrote had to do with the deception on preservation by the brethren at Bob Jones University (BJU). It is called: *Fundamentalist Deception on Bible Preservation.* It analyzed the BJU-sponsored *God's Word in our Hands–the Bible Preserved for Us.* J. B. Williams and Randolph Shaylor are the general and managing editors. Six of the seven members of the "Text and Translation Committee" are connected to BJU. It was published in March, 2003. This book has only the appearance of being true when it comes to Bible preservation. Hence the deception. Dr. Waite lists 334 deceptions found in *God's Word in Our Hands*. (GWOH)
We will list two of the deceptions here:
Deception #28, on page xxi, *"we have the word of God,"* Randolph Shaylor (BJU graduate) says:
"We believe that the Bible teaches that God has providentially preserved His written word. This preservation exists in the totality of the ancient manuscripts of that revelation. We are therefore certain that we possess the very word of God."

Truth #28.

That's what Randolph Shaylor (the managing editor of this book and a graduate from Bob Jones University) printed in the introductory pages. He defines some of the things. Where is the word of God preserved? If it is preserved "in the totality of ancient manuscripts," how can it be "God's word in our hands"? You can't go to the far-flung fields of the world to read God's word. We believe that God has preserved His Hebrew and His Greek Words and the most accurate translation of those preserved Words is the King James Bible.

Deception #31 on page xxii, *"we have the word of God,"* Randolph Shaylor (BJU graduate) says: under "written Word,"

"God has not chosen to preserve every word which He has spoken by audible voice through His prophets. He has chosen to convey the message of His person, purpose, glory, and works in written form."

Truth #31.

Notice the word, "message." Now the original inscripturation, "God's word has not passed away. He preserves the truth that he gave us in a form that is consistent with the original writing". Now, notice these special words: "form", the "truth," and so on. Here we have the word very illusive not the words are preserved, but the "message" and the "truth". [11]

The third and final book to be mentioned, written by those connected to Bob Jones University, is *Bible Preservation and the Providence of God*. This was answered by Dr. Waite in the book, *Bob Jones University's Error on Bible Preservation*. One of the authors of BPPG is Sam Schnaiter, at that time chairman of the Ancient Languages Department of BJU. Ron Tagliapietra is the second author and was at the staff at BJU.

This book continues the same line of deception as does *God's Word in Our Hands*, concerning Bible preservation. That is, it is against true Bible preservation. Samuel Schnaiter first stated this anti-true Biblical preservation stance at BJU back in the 1980's with his doctoral dissertation. The influence that this false position of BJU has had on the whole of Christendom, must be corrected. The presented truth to preservation of the correct original Hebrew, Aramaic, and Greek Words underlying the King James Bible, is the true preservation stance needed for this correction. Just like the stock market grows at too fast a rate needing a correction, this is what is hoped for in this situation.

As for the previously mentioned Ph.D. dissertation of Dr. Schnaiter from May of 1980, he makes these statements:

> *"This* (Greek N.T.) *text has been substantially preserved to this day."* (p. 155)
>
> *"The Scriptures...and the evidence we have require us to believe no more than that God has kept His message inviolate to the present day."* (p. 178)
>
> *"But no one today is in a position to know for a fact what the 'pure' text is among the variants of the New Testament manuscripts."* (p. 185)

This is outright denial of true Bible preservation. We believe we do have the pure text in the Hebrew and Aramaic Masoretic text and the New Testament Textus Receptus. We believe that this is God's true Bible text preservation of the underlying Words for the King James Bible. This is the correction to and the antidote for this present distorted situation on Bible preservation.

Back to the critique of BPPG, Dr. Waite states the fact that at least 212 false statements appear. They lead off the book by attacking and distorting the doctrine of the Bible. They do not talk about "preservation" they do not talk about "Scripture." They do not talk about the "Words" of Scripture. They do not believe that those "Words" of Scripture have been preserved to today.

Statement #18: p. 14.

"...issues discussed in units 2 and 3 also because they provide evidence that God has indeed preserved His word as He promised."

Comment#18:

That is the first red flag. When you see in their book the words, "preserved His word," do not dare believe they mean God has preserved His original Hebrew, Aramaic, and Greek words. ...they believe it ("word") means only the "ideas, thoughts, concepts, message, truth or teachings," but not the original words. They have added to the meaning of the word, word. In the Bible, whenever God talks about the word of God He means the Words of God. These two terms are co-equal. They are coextensive.

Statement #20: p. 16.

"Jesus said thy word is truth (John 17:17) which makes it infallible. It is inerrant or free from error because God cannot lie."

Comment #20:

I agree with that statement if "word" is properly defined as "words." I would disagree if the authors put their false definition on it as merely the "ideas, thoughts, concepts, message, truth, or teachings," but not the original Hebrew,

*Aramaic, and Greek words. Furthermore, since
they find errors in the words of Hebrew,
Aramaic, and Greek that we have today, how can
they be certain that the original words were
either "infallible" or "inerrant" except by faith?*

Statement #21: p. 16. [They are referring to John
10:35 b]

*"A document with errors can certainly be
"broken."*

Comment #21:

*I would agree with that. If the "Scripture cannot
be broken," this is a reference to perfect
plenary, verbal preservation of the original
words. It cannot refer, as they make it refer, only
to God's "ideas, thoughts, concepts, message,
truth, or teachings," I do not believe the writers
are applying accurately John 10:35b to this
subject.* [12]

The Bible is full of verses that God will perfectly preserve
His Words. In today's embroiled warfare over the extent and
means of Bible preservation, the widespread potential for
devastation exists to fundamental Christianity. The argument
has very plainly been stated to Biblical Christians for the verbal,
plenary inspiration and verbal, plenary preservation for the
Hebrew, Aramaic, and Greek Words underlying the King James
Bible. Some Fundamentalists recklessly believe that God has
promised to preserve His ideas, thoughts, concepts, message,
truth, or teachings, but not His Words. Those sincere
Fundamentalists in that camp deny God's preservation of His
Words in part or whole, and believe man's duty is to restore and
reconstruct God's Words, since they believe He has not
perfectly preserved them.

This type of position is rationalistic, prideful, and
destructive by its influence, to the faith of individual Christians

concerning the authority of Scripture.

> *Now I beseech you, brethren, mark them, which*
> *cause divisions and offences contrary to the*
> *doctrine which ye have learned; and avoid*
> *them."* (Romans 16:17)

If these Modern Textual Critics and Fundamentalists have distorted, misinformed, and deceived us about the doctrines of inspiration and preservation, what have they done to other doctrines through their Modern Bible Versions? We are soon to find out.

Chapter 7
Failure Alert!

Four Modern Versions

In this chapter we will look at four out of the top ten Modern Versions in use today. The four of choice will be: The New International Version (NIV); New American Standard Version (NASB); English Standard Version (ESV); and the Contemporary English Version (CEV).

These four Modern Versions are simply horrible translations for a myriad of reasons. No true Bible-believing Christian has any business dabbling in any of these per-versions. Much has been written on all of these so-called Bibles, so it is the duty of Bible-believers to study why they are so bad. What is presented here will only serve as an outline and a basis for pointing the serious student of the Words of God in the right direction.

The main reasons these per-versions are so bad are these: 1) They are all based on faulty Old Testament and New Testament texts; 2) They use the wrong translating techniques; 3) They have, compared to the King James Bible, inferior translators; and finally 4) inferior theology.

It is number four that we are concerned with in this chapter due to the fact that over 356 doctrines are affected by each modern translation. There is much denial in Christendom about this fact, (that doctrines are affected by Modern Versions), but the secret is already out. So many of the doctrines have been affected by Satan and all his translating cohorts, that the translations today can all be classified as total failures. The question has been raised whether or not a Christian should use any of the failed Modern Versions. It is always answered with an emphatic – NO!

The question should not be whether or not a Christian should use a perversion, but that all Christians should be united in sounding loud warnings against such usage. Doctrines directly affected by Modern Version committees will be discussed and highlighted.

Law of First-Mention

I mention the laws of first-mention because in a way they will be used in pointing out the failure of doctrine in the Modern Versions. The law or principle of first-mention will be used as a launching point presenting the earliest perversion of a Bible doctrine that can be found. It will be solely employed for the New Testament unless designated otherwise.

The law of "first-mention" is the principle in the interpretation of Scripture which states that the first mention or occurrence of a subject in Scripture establishes an unchangeable pattern, with that subject remaining unchanged in the mind of God throughout Scripture.[1]

Although we are not interpreting Scripture, per se, we are using this rule in order to find out if the Modern Versions pervert doctrines at the very first verse where a particular doctrine begins. If God wanted a doctrine to be understood by man, and if an unchangeable pattern was the design, who is man to come along and disrupt God's intentions? Remember, we are not defining the significance or scope, or developing a progressively advanced truth. We are merely seeking out and exposing doctrinal failure throughout the Modern Versions.

The Four Per-Versions
1. The NIV (New International Version)

The New International Version was, in the words of James Powell, President of the International Bible Society, (now Biblical)

> *"really God's project...His fingerprints are all over it, from the original dream to the final production."*[2]

The NIV is widely used in colleges, in churches of many denominations, and in the pulpit. Bookstores claim that it outsells the King James Bible or anything else that calls itself a Bible Version.

While many of the Modern Versions claim either to be translated literally or have excellent readability, the NIV claims both. It is true that the NIV can lay claim to the readability of its translation. It reads like a newspaper. The NIV's literalness though, is called into serious question, and has come under increasing scrutiny.

It's History

This Bible translation was begun in 1965 as an idea at a meeting in Palos Heights, Illinois, at the Trinity Christian College. Members of the Reformed Church, National Association of Evangelicals (NAE), and a group of international scholars hatched the idea. The Biblical Society was to do the translation. A New Testament was released in 1973, and an Old Testament and Complete Bible was released in 1978. In 1996 a New International Readers Version (NIrV) was made into a gender inclusive version. However, a "Baptist uproar" killed the gender-neutral translation of the New International Version of the Bible.

Kenneth L. Barker, one of the NIV Translators, claimed that their goal "of course, is to be as accurate as possible".

Listed among the "NIV Facts" was " 4) Accuracy had the highest priority on the list of NIV goals."[3]

But, according to a rating section of "How Bible Scholars Rated the NIV, there was no rating on 'accuracy' "[4]

Textual Problems (Old Testament)

The NIV Manuscript base for the Old Testament was the Biblia Hebraica Stuttgartensia Hebrew Text. This is an abridged Hebrew text from only one Hebrew Manuscript, The Leningrad Manuscript (B19a or "L"), (1008 A.D.), edited by Ben Asher. This manuscript was first used in Kittel's 1937 Edition Biblia Hebraica Stuttgartensia. There are 20,000 to 30,000 footnote suggested changes to the original Hebrew Masoretic text up to that time. This altered Hebrew text is used in all Modern Versions. Along with the corrupted Stuttgartensia Hebrew Text, the NIV also based their Old Testament on the foundation of:

(1)   Dead Sea Scrolls.
(2)   Samaritan Pentateuch
(3)   Ancient Scribal Traditions
(4)   Variant Hebrew-reading in the margin
(5)   Consonantal Texts
(6)   Early Versions
(7)   Septuagint (OT translated into Greek)
(8)   Symmachus (Greek version of OT)
(9)   Theodotion (translated Hebrew Bible into Greek)
(10)   Vulgate (Latin translation)
(11)   Syriac Peshitta
(12)   Targums (Paraphrases in Aramaic)
(13)   Juxta Hebraica (of Jerome) (for the Psalms)
(14)   Different set of vowels (instances)[5]

A Different Greek Text Used

By their own admission, the NIV did not use the Received Text or Textus Receptus on which the King James Bible was based.

Although the NIV Translators were free to consider and incorporate readings from other Greek Texts (thus rendering the basis of the NIV New Testament an "eclectic" text), it appears that they followed the United Bible Society's (UBS) third edition for their New Testament Work.[6]

According to the online free encyclopedia, the NIV Translators also used the Nestle-Aland Greek text. Both the UBS and Nestle-Aland Greek texts have a spurious base of Vatican "B" and Aleph" (Sinai) texts, which Barker claims are *"up to 1,000 years older than those used by the King James."*[7] The fact is that the manuscripts used by the King James Translators date back to the very Autographs of Manuscripts. (See Appendix B).

Translation Technique Used in NIV

"The first concern of the Translators has been the Accuracy of the Translation and its fidelity to the thought of the Biblical writers... Because thought patterns and syntax differ from language to language, faithful communication of the meaning of the writers of the Bible demands frequent modifications in sentence structure and constant regard for the Contextual meanings of words." [8]

"This 'fidelity to the thought' is, per se, 'Dynamic Equivalency' rather than 'verbal, or form equivalency' such as the King James Bible has used."[9]

Dynamic Equivalence Defined

The primary target of Dynamic Equivalence is to make the message of Scripture culturally understandable by every man and woman in a particular language group. The people or receptors become the focus. This is wrong. The primary aim of any believer, translator included, is to glorify the Lord (Revelation 4:11; Isaiah 42.8). There is nothing more important to the Lord than to make His Words known, because salvation comes by faith in the finished work of the Lord, and faith comes by His Words (Romans 10:17). Neither is the target of Dynamic Equivalence justified because contact with remote Language-groups is now possible. Language-groups are not new. Language-groups began at the Tower of Babel (Genesis 11:9).[10]

Dynamic Equivalence is employed when words in the text are either added, subtracted, or changed in some other way.

The Translating Technique of Dynamic Equivalence was the brainchild of Eugene Nida. A little bit of his mind set is apparent in his statement: "the Scriptures must be intelligible to non-Christians, and if they are, they will also be intelligible to Christians."[11]

Nida, who knows better now, made his works to be more appealing to book advertisers, publishers, and scholars; lifting translator's reputations in the eyes of the world; and supporting the world's false understanding of God's book.

The Failures: Omissions, Additions, and Changes

You will hear people say that the Westcott-Hort Text, the basis for today's UBS and Nestle-Aland Greek texts, has some omissions, additions, and changes. Then they will tell you that no doctrines are involved. But there are doctrines affected, and major ones too. Then they say you can take out a verse with doctrine and assure you it is found elsewhere in the New

Testament. When that is done in the NIV and any other of the Modern Versions, that Version whether it be Greek, English, or Urdu, is a failed Version.

It can be proven that Bible Corrupters and heretics, we can call then Gnostics, took things out of the Greek manuscripts. They did this to conform to their own corrupted theology. This happened mainly in the first hundred years after the originals were penned. However, they only did this butchery with the manuscripts they could get their hands on.

Since it is the Westcott and Hort Greek type text that is in error, it can be shown that doctrines are affected in today's Modern Versions. If only one doctrine, in one place can be shown to be affected, then that Modern Version is deemed a failure. It may seem to be a harsh test, but all doctrines are kept entirely intact in the King James Bible. The King James Bible is the standard by which all other per-versions are to be measured. Doctrines will be shown to be affected and all Modern Versions based on the Westcott-Hort Greek text are failed Versions.

Doctrine

Doctrine simply means teaching, but the biblical usage refers to sound teaching based on the Words of God.[12]

The Doctrinal Passages

Five different categories of doctrines will be examined and challenged in the Modern Versions.

1) Theology Proper (Doctrine of God).
2) Christology (Doctrine of Jesus Christ).
3) Pneumatology (Doctrine of the Holy Spirit).
4) Bibliology (Doctrine of the Bible).
5) Soteriology (Doctrine of Salvation).

Once again, the four Modern Versions being examined are:

1) New International Version (N.I.V.).
2) New American Standard Version (N.A.S.V.).

3) English Standard Version (E.S.V.).
4) Contemporary English Version (C.E.V.).
Doctrinal Failures in the N.I.V.
1) Theology Proper (Doctrine of God)

a) *"But seek ye first the kingdom <u>of God</u>, and his righteousness; and all these things shall be added unto you."* (Matthew 6:30)

This is the first instance in the New Testament of any dynamic equivalence as it relates to God. This removal of God follows Vatican B and Aleph manuscripts. This is a failure of doctrine and proves the Textus Receptus and the King James Bible as doctrinally second to none.

b) *"And he said unto him, Why callest thou me good? There is none good but one, that is, <u>God</u>: but if thou wilt enter into life, keep the Commandments."* (Matthew 19:17)

The removal of the word, God, and changing His Name to "one" definitely changes the doctrine of God and His goodness. The NIV follows B and Aleph again. This is an obvious failure of doctrine, proving the Textus Receptus and the King James Bible as the best.

c) *"For in the resurrection they neither marry, nor are given in marriage, but are as the angels <u>of God</u> in heaven."* (Matthew 22:30)

The underlined words, *"of God,"* are removed in the NIV because of following the B and Aleph false texts. This is a serious breach of the doctrine of God and His Creation. This is yet another failure of doctrine, proving the Textus Receptus and the King James Bible unequaled.

d) *". . . Grace be unto you, and peace, <u>from God our Father, and the Lord Jesus Christ</u>."* (1 Thessalonians 1:1)

"From God our Father, and the Lord Jesus Christ," are omitted and deny the goodness of God the Father and the Lord Jesus Christ, in providing grace and peace. These refer to the moral attributes of God which are eternal and unchangeable.

Any change would imply that God is imperfect in His attributes or that He is somehow not perfect now. This is a gross failure of doctrine Proper in the NIV and proves the Textus Receptus and the King James Bible unsurpassed.

e) *"for there are three that bear record <u>in heaven, the Father, the Word, and the Holy Ghost; and these three are one, And there are three that bear witness in earth</u>, the Spirit, and the water, and the blood: and these three agree in one."* (1 John 5:7,8)

This is the threefold witness, and the clearest reference to the Trinity of God in all the Scriptures. According to Dr. Moorman, removing these words (underlined) leaves a gender mismatch in the Greek. For a full defence of this Trinitarian passage, see KJMVT, p. 115. This is a blatant proof of doctrinal mishandling and failure, once again proving the Textus Receptus and the King James Bible unexcelled in doctrine.

It becomes rather obvious that the NIV is a failed Translation. But there are four more doctrines to explore.

2) Christology (Doctrine of Christ)

a) *"And knew her not till she had brought forth her <u>firstborn</u> son: and he called his name JESUS."* (Matthew 1:25)

Here indeed is a very early omitted doctrine in Matthew, the very first book of the New Testament. By using the phrase *"to a son,"* instead of *"firstborn"* son, Mary may have had other children which could be implied. The word "firstborn" does not limit Mary to only one son, as was the case when she had other sons. This is in direct refutation of the Roman Catholic's false doctrine of Mary's perpetual virginity. In point of fact, this is very serious doctrinal failure exhibited by the NIV, proving that the Textus Receptus and the King James Bible are second to none.

b) *"<u>For the Son of man is come to save that which was lost</u>."* (Matthew 18:11)

This entire verse is omitted in the NIV. It is not there. This is missing in Manuscripts B and Aleph which the Modern Versions follow in translation. This doctrine, as is any doctrine, is important because it defines the Lord Jesus Christ's mission to earth. This is very clear and is easily understandable. This is complete doctrinal failure on the part of the NIV and keeps proving that the Textus Receptus and the King James Bible are the best.

c) *"Therefore being a prophet, and knowing that God had sworn with an oath to him, that the fruit of his loins, <u>according to the flesh, he would raise up Christ,</u> to sit on his throne;"* (Acts 2:30)

Having eliminated the underlined words, the Scripture cutters proceeded to deny the bodily resurrection of the Lord Jesus Christ. Both major Corrupted Manuscripts, Aleph and Vatican B are followed. Anyone, most likely the Great Usurper, could occupy His throne, denying that the Lord Jesus Christ will also return in the flesh. This is great blasphemy, the thoughts of apostates and severe doctrinal failure by the NIV. This further proves the Textus Receptus and the King James Bible unequaled.

d) *"And to make all men see what is the fellowship of the mystery, which from the beginning of the world hath been hid in God, who created all things <u>by Jesus Christ</u>."* (Ephesians 3:9)

By outright eliminating the Words, *"by Jesus Christ,"* manuscripts Aleph and Vatican B and the NIV attempt to sweep away the Deity of our Lord Jesus Christ. This is doctrinal failure and wickedness, supporting the fact that the Textus Receptus and the King James Bible are unsurpassed.

e) *"Saying, we give thee thanks, O Lord God Almighty, which art, and wast, <u>and art to come</u>;"* (Revelation 11:17)

"And art to come," is non-existent in Aleph (no B in Revelation) and in the NIV, which affects the doctrine of the Lord Jesus Christ's return to earth future. This is serious

doctrinal failure, for it also implies the Gnostic belief that the Lord Jesus Christ was a mere man and not God, and therefore did and does not have the power to return or fulfill His promises. This bolsters the belief that the Textus Receptus and the King James Bible are unexcelled in doctrine.

3) Pneumatology (Doctrine of the Holy Spirit)

a) "(*For the fruit of the <u>Spirit</u> is in all goodness and righteousness and truth;)*" (Ephesians 5:9)

Manuscripts B and Aleph change the Word "Spirit." Fruit of the "Light" is not the Holy Spirit in all goodness. This is doctrinal failure in the false Greek texts and the NIV. This shows the Textus Receptus and the King James Bible as the best.

b) "*For we are the Circumcision, which worship <u>God in the Spirit</u>,*" (Philippians 3:3)

B and Aleph and the NIV change "God in the Spirit" to "who worship by the Spirit of God." We have a failure of doctrine by the Modern Version by not including the object of our worship and that we worship God in the Spirit, since the Spirit is in us. Once again, the Textus Receptus and the King James Bible have it right.

4) Bibliology (Doctrine of the Bible)

a) The Total deletion of the last 12 verses of Mark 16.

9. "Now when Jesus was risen early the first day of the week, he appeared first to Mary Magdalene, out of whom he had cast seven devils."

10. "And she went and told them that had been with him, as they mourned and wept."

11. "And they, when they had heard that he was alive, and had been seen of her, believed not."

12. "After that he appeared in another form unto two of them, as they walked, and went into the country."

13. "And they went and told it unto the residue: neither believed they them."

14. "Afterward he appeared unto the eleven as they sat at meat, and upbraided them with their unbelief and hardness of heart, because they believed not them which had seen him after he was risen."

15. "And he said unto them, Go ye into all the world, and preach the gospel to every creature."

16. "He that believeth and is baptized shall be saved; but he that believeth not shall be damned."

17. "And these signs shall follow them that believe; In my name shall they cast out devils; they shall speak with new tongues;"

18. "They shall take up serpents; and if they drink any deadly thing, it shall not hurt them; they shall lay hands on the sick, and they shall recover."

19. "So then after the Lord had spoken unto them, he was received up into heaven, and sat on the right hand of God."

20. "And they went forth, and preached every where, the Lord working with them, and confirming the word with signs following. Amen."

The NIV completely omits Mark 16:9-20. This follows the Greek texts of B and Aleph. This is horrendous doctrinal failure to believe the overwhelming evidence that this passage in Mark is genuine. This only proves the Textus Receptus and the King James Bible as supreme.

5) Soteriology (Doctrine of Salvation)

a) *"But go ye and learn what that meaneth, I will have mercy, and not sacrifice: for I am not come to call the righteous, but sinners to repentance.* (Matthew 9:13)

By not including the Words *"to repentance,"* the NIV stops the gospel short, thus rendering the means to salvation changed according to the Translators' own interpretation. This is affected doctrine and is a failure, thus insuring the Textus Receptus and the King James Bible as being far superior.

Thus, after closer examination of the NIV, which is filled

with paraphrases and Dynamic Equivalence (over 6,653 instances), it would be neglectful to not deem the New International Version a failed Version. ALL Christians need to be warned of the dangers of using such a per-version.

2. The NASV (New American Standard Version)

The New American Standard Version is the second in our series of four per-versions of the Bible. It is also based in the New Testament on the Westcott-Hort-type Greek text. This is in the form of the Nestle-Aland (NA) text that differs from the Received Text in over 5,600 places and involving almost 10,000 Greek words.

It is puzzling why so many fundamentalist brethren recommend this Bible Version over the King James Bible. This effort is led by members of the Fundamentalist Baptist Fellowship (FBF) and Bob Jones University (BJU). The NASV was a rescue operation by the Lockman Foundation (for whom BJU faculty consulted). The Lockman Foundation (LF) began in 1942 by F. Dewey Lockman. It is responsible for the translation, publication, and distribution of the NASB, the Amplified Bible, and two Spanish Bibles, a Korean Standard Bible, a Chinese Bible, and a new Hindi (India) Bible. The NASV was updated in 1995.

Philosophy

As mentioned, the NASV project was a rescue mission of the flagging American Standard Version (ASV). They tout themselves as the MOST literally translated of the 20th Century. One of their "Fourfold aims" was to be true to the original Hebrew, Aramaic, and Greek. There is not any way that this could have been achieved knowing the philosophy of the Translators. They did not believe in the preservation of the Hebrew Masoretic and Greek Textus Receptus Bible Words. The Translators favored a rationalistic stance when it came to the texts. They believed that the historical evidence of the manuscripts is favored over faith in God to perfectly preserve His Words. The pro-NASV-ites constantly brought into question the integrity and accuracy of the King James Bible and its underlying Words. In treating the Bible and its Words as any other book, the NASV's Translators deny the New Testament Received Text theology (1 Thessalonians 2:13). They have followed Westcott and Hort's unbiblical approach in this and also the fact that they believed that the texts were not tampered with by any heretics. This is also refuted by the Bible in Peter's Epistle (II Peter 3:16).

Textual Problems

The New American Standard Version (NASV) admits in their preface which inferior Hebrew texts they used.

> *"Hebrew text: In the present translation the latest edition of 1) Rudolph Kittel's BIBLIA HEBRAICA has been employed together with the most recent 2) light from Lexicography, 3) Cognate Languages, and 4) the Dead Sea Scrolls."*[13]

They do use, along with others, the Hebrew Masoretic text. The Kittel Hebrew text they use is the 1937 edition. We need to know that this Kittel text has fifteen to twenty suggested changes to the Masoretic texts, placed in the footnotes on every page. This amounts to over 20,000 changes to the Old Testament.

In the New Testament, the Nestle-Aland Novum Testamentum Graece was used. This text has more than 8,000 differences compared to the New Testament Words used in the King James Bible. The producers of the NASV New Testament are not interested in the doctrine of inerrancy in the originals. This unbelieving view is advanced by Daniel B. Wallace who states: (Defending errant manuscripts B and Aleph) that textual critics *"have sufficient respect for a biblical author that they will not impute to him an ostensible inaccuracy unless the manuscript testimony compels them to do so. At all points, textual critics are historians who have to base their views on data, not mere theological convictions."*[14]

He goes on,

"whatever one's beliefs about inerrancy, it seems to me, they have to adjust to this piece of evidence."[15]

So, we are to abandon all sound reasoning on Textual matters, to accept the ancient notion of an errant B and Aleph over an inerrant Biblical writer, in this case Mark. Biblical Christians who are defending the Critical Text and Modern Versions, such as the NASV, must know that they defend the unbelieving view of the doctrine of inerrancy.

Techniques of Translation

Is the Modern Version NASV better than the King James Bible based on its translation techniques? They claim to have Translated according to a Formal Equivalence Technique. However, Dr. D. A. Waite found over 4,000 examples of Dynamic Equivalence (additions, subtractions, and changes) regarding the Words of God. How can this be? The NASV uses italics occasionally when it suited them when they departed from the Hebrew or Greek. They added, subtracted, and changed so many words, one does not know what the original words are. This does not sound like a formal equivalence Translation. No, the problem is that they have purposefully adopted a non-verbal equivalence type of translation, and non-formal, non-literal equivalence types of translation. They did not use a word-for-word method, using the Hebrew and Greek Words to equal the words in English. If they did use a formal type of equivalence for example, the nouns, adjectives, prepositions, participles, verbs, and so on, these would have been rendered from the Hebrew and the Greek to the English in the same way, with the same forms of the language. This is not what has happened in the NASV or in any of the Modern Versions today. They have transformed the grammar, changing everything from one form to another. If you believe every Word from God is important you will not believe as the Dynamic Equivalence people do.

Doctrinal Failures in the NASV

1) Theology Proper (Doctrine of God)

a) "*He went away again the second time, and prayed, saying, O my Father, if this cup may not pass away from me, except I drink it, thy will be done.*" (Matthew 26:42)

Following B and Aleph, omitting the Word "cup" from this verse does not make sense in the NASV. What is the will of the Father, if it isn't the cup of the wrath of sins by mankind. That is not indicated here. This is doctrinal failure and the Textus Receptus and the King James Bible remain unexcelled.

b) "*But if ye do not forgive, neither will your Father which is in heaven forgive your trespasses.*" (Mark 11:26)

This is a promise of God. This is an attribute of a perfect God. This is a weakening of the doctrine of God and the NASV has erred by following the errant manuscripts of B and Aleph. The NASV puts silly brackets around this verse, raising doubts as to its genuineness and integrity as part of the text. This is flagrant doctrinal error and proves the Textus Receptus and The King James Bible as unsurpassed.

2) Christology (Doctrine of Christ)

a) "*Now when Jesus had heard that John was cast into prison, he departed into Galilee;*" (Matthew 4:12)

Here is a very early instance of the failure of the NASV when it concerns our Lord Jesus Christ. The illuminated translators of the NASV removed "Jesus" from giving the prophecy of the great light. Who they expected to do so is not clear. This is clearly doctrinal failure, for the NASV followed manuscripts B and Aleph. This further proves that the Textus Receptus and the King James Bible are the best.

b)   "*and Jesus, walking by the Sea of Galilee, saw two brethren, Simon called Peter, and Andrew his brother, casting a net into the sea: for they were fishers.*" (Matthew 4:18)

"*Jesus*" is removed by the NASV translators, following B and Aleph, the two main errant manuscripts. Who they believe is the Saviour calling these two to discipleship is anybody's best guess. This is a ridiculous doctrinal failure in the NASV and its corrupted texts, and only proves the Textus Receptus and the King James Bible as unequaled.

3) Pneumatology (Doctrine of the Holy Spirit)

a) "*Even the Spirit of truth; whom the world cannot receive, because it seeth him not, neither knoweth him: but ye know him; for he dwelleth with you, and shall be in you.*" (John 14:17)

Manuscripts P66 and B read "and is," and so the NASV carries this error in its text. The fact is, the Holy ministry of the Holy Ghost dwelling in us was still in the future when this Scripture was written. This is doctrinal error and proves still the fact that the Textus Receptus and the King James Bible are supreme.

4) Bibliology (Doctrine of the Bible)

a) "*And he said unto them, Unto you it is given to know the mystery of the kingdom of God: but unto them that are without, all these things are done in parables.*" (Mark 4:11)

The NASV goes along with B and Aleph and drops the "to know" phrase. The mystery has to have been forwarded by Christ's action of teaching, not just any mystery other than those found in the Gospel. This is dangerous wording. This is dangerous doctrinal failure and supports the superiority of the Textus Receptus and the King James Bible.

5) Soteriology (Doctrine of Salvation)

a) *"That whosoever believeth in him should not perish, but have eternal life."* (John 3:15)

Aleph and B once again lead the way that the NASV follows in perverting the doctrine of salvation. This is doctrinal failure in the NASV and its errant texts, confirming that the Textus Receptus and the King James Bible are the best.

b) *"No man hath seen God at any time; the only begotten Son, which is in the bosom of the Father, he hath declared him."* (John 1:18)

The omission of Son, and substitution of God would deny us salvation if the Lord Jesus Christ was not begotten and came to earth. This verse with the Word for "Son" being deleted is Gnostic corruption in the classic sense. This is doctrinal failure in the NASV and its errant texts, and continues to prove the Textus Receptus and the King James Bible as the best.

Many good Christian leaders have been forewarned about the erroneous promises made about the NASV. These have been the promises that the NASV is more accurate and up-to-date, making it somehow better than the King James Bible. But if dear Christians will pay even the slightest attention to the English that has been given them by the scholars behind this modern per-version, they would not be confident that he or she possesses a complete and accurate Bible. This Version differs greatly from the King James Bible in so many places that a choice would have to be made in one direction or the other. Simply, the NASV is a failed version.

3. The E.S.V. (English Standard Version)

Work on the English Standard Version (ESV) with Apocrypha, began in the 1990's by Dr. Lane T. Dennis. He stated, most remarkably, that there was a need for a new literal translation. The ESV is a warmed over Translation of the 1971 Revised Standard Version (RSV) which is 6% revised and the rest RSV.

The ESV is adapted from the Revised Standard Version of the Bible, Copyright Division of Christian Education of the National Council of Churches of Christ in the USA. All rights reserved.[16]

Crossway/Good News Publishers of the ESV pays a quarterly fee to the NCCC. The NCCC, from which the RSV Copyright was obtained, is an apostate organization. As an example of their handiwork, the NCCC has accepted homosexual denominations into their membership. They do not faithfully support traditional marriage. Their work and fellowship with leftist and Communist regimes is well known and documented. The Family Tree of this version is interesting.

History of Version

The English Standard Version is a revised and updated version of the old American Standard Version which came out in 1901 and was revised (RSV) in 1952 and updated in 197. It was the 1971 updated Revised Standard Version (RSV) which was used plus the 6% revision to make the ESV. If that isn't confusing enough, the new American Standard Version (NASV) and the Revised Standard Version both take their parentage from the 1901 ASV which was the American Version of the Westcott + Hort 1881 English Revised Version. It looks something like this:

ERV (1881)
ASV (1901)
Revised Standard Version (RSV) (1952) (1971 Revision)
Amplified Bible (AB) (1965)
New American Standard Bible (NASB) (1971)
New Revised Standard Version   ESV (2001)
NRSV (1990)

After the introduction of the Revised Standard Version in 1971, another Version was needed to overcome the gender-inclusive language controversy it had stirred up. It corrected some accuracies, cleaned up some of its language, and of course, self-proclaimed itself to be more literal a translation. Since there already was a New Revised Standard Version, the name English Standard Version (ESV) was agreed upon.

Translating Philosophy

The Translation team addressed three areas that were to overcome criticisms against many recent Modern Versions. These are listed in the Preface to the ESV.

The ESV was to be a "literal" translation. It was intended to have a more weighted "word-for-word" style translation opening a window into the structure and meaning of the original Words using current literary English. They admit to capturing the "echoes" and "overtones of meaning" and not outright rejecting "functional equivalence," updated parlance for the archaic "Dynamic Equivalence."

In the spirit of retaining Christian doctrine intact, a straining was needed to continue use of theological terms. They generously used words such as grace, faith, justification, sanctification, redemption, regeneration, reconciliation, and propitiation.   After all, they're just words, and a reaction anyway to address criticisms.

And then in the area of gender inclusive language, great pains were taken to accommodate by using "anyone" to replace "any man," and "people" instead of "men," when the original refers to both men and women. But there are many, many of the original gender exclusive terms they just did not bother with.

To the degree that Dynamic Equivalence (Functional Equivalence to the ESV) is used is much greater than is stated in the preface. There is more or less a fairly large discrepancy between what was advertised and what the ESV actually turned out to be. But this is beyond the scope of this study, and left to explore. Suffice it to say that words are added, (2 Corinthians 4:3; Ephesians 3:6; 1 Timothy 5:21; Hebrews 6:10), Words and verses subtracted, Word orders changed, and verb forms and tenses changed. There are Idiomatic Equivalents throughout and throw in some "awkward" English to boot. That is the very definition of Dynamic Equivalence (Functional Equivalence to the ESV); adding, subtracting, and changing Words in the Bible.

In 1975 the World Council of Churches at Nairobi adopted this same method (Dynamic Equivalence; Functional equivalence to the ESV) as the method of translation. They followed Eugene Nida, the father of Dynamic Equivalence, and they followed the United Bible Society and the American Bible Society.[17]

About their alleged "Literal" Translating: "a translator must not be caught doubting any 'jot or tittle' of the Scriptures or its literal interpretation. Words must be translated from the source-language into the receptor-language without the translator's influence of him on interpretation."[18]

If words are changed, meanings are changed. Words need to have the same exact basic meaning they would have in normal usage. By using Functional Equivalence the ESV Translators abandoned the right use of the Words given by God, and thus are not all rendered correctly in the receptor-language, in our case English.

This does not back up the ESV Translators' attempts to correct the very liberal RSV and convert the ESV into a conservative translation. They failed in this mission, as the version they created cannot be relied on as trustworthy for Bible-believing Christians.

Textual Basis

Understanding that the ESV is more than 90% of the deficient Revised Standard Version (RSV) of the 1971 revision, its translators were made up of those who rejected the Verbal, Plenary Inspiration of the Bible. Of these, Dr. Bruce Metzger was one of the 32 members of the RSV (1952) committee. His apostate beliefs are more well known to all today, but let's

review.   Metzger was quoted in the RSV introduction as
follows:
"The events in the Old Testament from the creation to the
Conquest of the Promised Land were out of a matrix of myth,
legend, and history."   He did not believe in a literal
interpretation of the entire Pentateuch.

He thought very low of the book of Job saying it came to us
from *"ancient folklore, circulated among oriental sages in the
2nd millennium, B.C."* Metzger thought the book of Jonah was
a popular legend. In 1989 Metzger was Translation Committee
Chairman for the New Revised Standard Version (NRSV). It
was reviewed to have retained all the flaws of the old RSV and
brought out new ones of its own.

The textual basis does not grow out of the "Tyndale-King
James Legacy," as the authors suggest. The Hebrew text of the
ESV is based on a Masoretic text found in the Biblia Hebraica
Stuttgartensia (2 ed., 1983).   This text is from Stuttgart
Germany, 1967/77.   This is a newer version of the Kittel
Hebraica of 1937. This text is not the same that underlies the
King James Bible. This is the Ben Asher type Masoretic Text
instead of the Ben Chayyim Hebrew Masoretic text. The Ben
Asher Text (used in ESV) follows the Leningrad Manuscript
(B19 or "L").

Its Hebrew Masoretic text appears on top of the page,
where 15–20 suggested changes in the text appear as footnotes.
All together it totals 20,000 – 30,000 changes in the Old
Testament. They also consulted
> *"The Dead Sea Scrolls, the Septuagint, the
> Samaritan Pentateuch, the Syriac Peshitta,
> the Latin Vulgate, and other sources."*[19]

The Greek text used the 1993 editions of the United Bible
Societies (UBS) Greek text and the NOVUM Testamentum
Graece (27th ed.), Nestle-Aland Greek text. In a few places the

ESV followed a Greek text different than the UBS 4th ed., or Nestle-Aland 27th ed., unspecified.

The Greek text used by the ESV, is essentially the Westcott–Hort text, objections acknowledged, a text which differs in 8000 places from the Textus Receptus as stated by Dr. Jack Moorman. It is 2886 words (Greek) shorter than the TR, affecting 356 doctrinal passages.

Doctrinal Failures in the ESV
1) Theology Proper (Doctrine of God)

a) *"And Joseph and his mother marveled at those things which were spoken of him."* (Luke 2:33)

The Modern Versions follow B and Aleph here. Joseph is substituted as the Jesus' "Father." Joseph was not the Father of Jesus. "Joseph" is the correct Word to be used in this verse. This is doctrinal failure of the ESV and its underlying texts and shows the Textus Receptus and the King James Bible as being much better.

b) *"but why dost thou judge thy brother? Or why dost thou set at naught thy brother? For we shall all stand before the judgment seat of Christ."* (Romans 14:10)

Again Vatican B and Sinai Aleph are the guilty manuscripts. It is not God's judgment seat that all born-again Christians will stand before. "The Father" judgeth no man, and it is false teaching to do so. This is doctrinal error in the ESV and the Textus Receptus and the King James Bible superior.

c) *"But if any man say unto you, this is offered in sacrifice unto idols, eat not for his sake that shewed it, and for conscience sake: for the earth is the Lord's, and the fullness thereof:"* (1 Corinthians 10:28)

This whole phrase is eliminated in the ESV which teaches that it is God's own creation and He has ownership. This is doctrinal failure in the ESV and the Textus Receptus and King James Bible unexcelled.

d) *"And without controversy great is the mystery of godliness; <u>God</u> was manifest in the flesh, justified in the Spirit, seen of angels, preached unto the Gentiles, believed on in the world, received up into glory."* 1 Timothy 3:16)

ESV says "He" instead of God. In their footnotes they pronounce the Greek as being "who." This gives away the fact they follow the errant Vatican Band Sinai Aleph manuscripts into doctrinal error. This proves once again the Textus Receptus and the King James Bible as being unequaled.

e) *"Blessed are they <u>that do his commandments</u>, that they may have right to the tree of life, and may enter in through the gates into the city.* (Revelation 22:14)

The Son refers to the Father as to His commandments that the Father said unto the Son to speak, in John 12:50. The Revised Version changes this to wash their robes while noting in their footnotes that some manuscripts have "do his commandments." B and Aleph do not have "do his commandments," and this is doctrinal failure carried down to the ESV and Modern Versions. The Textus Receptus and the King James Bible reign supreme.

2) Christology (Doctrine of Christ)

a) *"No man hath seen God at any time; the only begotten <u>Son</u>, which is the boson of the Father, he hath declared him."* (John 1:18)

B and Aleph, and most all the Modern Versions change Son to God, and the ESV follows suit. This follows Gnostic perversion of its doctrine of "other" gods along with the Lord Jesus Christ. Not having "Son" is serious doctrinal error which the ESV did not correct. The Textus Receptus and the King James Bible are the best.

b) *"For God so loved the world that he gave his only <u>begotten</u> Son, that whosoever believeth in him should not perish, but have everlasting life."* (John 3:16)

By eliminating "begotten" the ESV follows along with Vatican B and Aleph. "Begotten" signifies that the Lord Jesus Christ was the only one of His kind, to come forth of the Father as His Son. It explains the fact that the Lord Jesus Christ did not become, but was from everlasting the Son of God and God the Son. The ESV is in doctrinal error in this verse and proves that the Textus Receptus and the King James Bible are unsurpassed.

c) *"For this cause I bow my knees unto the Father of our Lord Jesus Christ."* (Ephesians 3:14)

The ESV deletes "of our Lord Jesus Christ" disconnecting Him from the "Father," weakening the Lord Jesus Christ's Deity. This is doctrinal error from B and Aleph, in the ESV and supports the superiority of the Textus Receptus and the King James Bible.

d) *"Who, being in the form of God, thought it not robbery to be equal with God:"* (Philippians 2:6)

Although the ESV includes both of the Words, "God," the change to the text to, *"did not count equality with God a thing to be grasped."* This coincides with the NIV's rendition of this verse, throwing a shadow and doubt on the deity of the Lord Jesus Christ. This is doctrinal error and it proves the Textus Receptus and the King James Bible as being far superior.

e) *"that ye be not soon shaken in mind, or be troubled, neither by spirit, nor by word, nor by letter as from us, as that the day of Christ is at hand."* (2 Thessalonians 2:2)

"Christ" is changed to "Lord" in the ESV, confusing the Rapture with the Day of the Lord which is from the beginning of the Tribulation until the end of the 1000 year Millennium. This is doctrinal error on the part of the ESV, proving the Textus Receptus and the King James Bible as the best.

f) *"Who being the brightness of his glory, and the express image of his person, and upholding all things by the word of his power, when he had by himself purged our sins, sat down on the right hand of the Majesty on high.*" (Hebrews 1:3)

Aleph and B do not have the Words to translate "by himself." The ESV picks this up and leaves them out of the verse. You need these Words to keep the doctrine that the Lord Jesus Christ did all the work on Calvary intact and not have a usurper take credit for dying for our sins. This is doctrinal error on the part of the ESV and keeps intact the superiority of the Textus Receptus and the King James Bible.

3) Pneumatology (Doctrine of the Holy Spirit)

a) "*There is therefore now no condemnation to them which are in Christ Jesus, who walk not after the flesh, but after the Spirit.*" (Romans 8:1)

The entire underlined phrase is left out of ESV. This follows Aleph and B. If we indeed have life in the Spirit, and He is our power to live that life in the Spirit, we need to know that. This deletion is doctrinal error against the Spirit of God and keeps proving that the Textus Receptus and the King James Bible are superior.

b) "*(For the fruit of the Spirit is in all goodness and righteousness and truth;)*" (Ephesians 5:9)

The ESV follows B and Aleph and changes "Spirit" to "Light". The fruit of the "Light" is not the name of the Holy Spirit. This is doctrinal failure in these false texts and shows the Textus Receptus and the King James Bible as unexcelled.

4) Bibliology (Doctrine of the Bible)

a) "*Howbeit this kind goeth not out but by prayer and fasting.*" (Matthew 17:21)

The entire verse is missing from the English Standard Version. This deletes doctrine completely from the inscripturated Words of Christ Jesus. This is doctrinal failure in the ESV and upholds the Textus Receptus and the King James Bible as the best.

b) *"And I say unto you, whosoever shall put away his wife, except it be for fornication, and shall marry another committeth adultery: and whoso marrieth her which is put away doth commit adultery."* (Matthew 19:9)

The ESV follows Aleph in deleting this phrase disrupting this doctrine and deleting inscripturated Words of God. This is doctrinal failure, with the Textus Receptus and the King James Bible unequaled.

c) *"Woe unto you, scribes and Pharisees, hypocrites! For ye devour widows houses, and for a pretense make long prayer: therefore ye shall receive the greater damnation."* (Matthew 23:14)

The ESV, B, and Aleph all drop this verse. There must be something about devouring widows' houses that the Bible mutilators don't need reminding of. This is woeful doctrinal failure and proves Textus Receptus and King James Version superiority.

d) *"Where their worm dieth not, and the fire is not quenched."* (Mark 9:44)

It is quite understandable why the makers of B and Aleph, and the ESV don't like this verse and this teaching. This is doctrinal failure and deletion of God's Holy Words. The Textus Receptus and the King James Bible remain on top.

e) *"And the scripture was fulfilled, which saith, And he was numbered with the transgressors."* (Mark 15:28)

This verse is completely missing in the ESV, as it is in B and Aleph, the errant manuscripts. This is deletion of God's Words and doctrine which is error. The Textus Receptus and King James Version are unequaled.

f) *"Two men shall be in the field; the one shall be taken, and the other left."* (Luke 17:36)

Most of the corrupt manuscripts do not have this verse, *"this verse is wanting."* This includes, naturally, B and Aleph and by extension the ESV. This important teaching on the second coming will not be learned by many. This is doctrinal failure and leaves intact the Textus Receptus and King James Version as being the best.

g)   *"As it is written <u>in the prophets,</u> Behold, I send my messenger before thy face, which shall prepare thy way before thee."* (Mark 1:2)

Hopefully by the next Modern Translation the translators will finally learn that this verse is not from Isaiah. Verse 2 of Mark is from Malachi 3:1. The next verse is from Isaiah 40:3; thus God's Words, "in the prophets." This is doctrinal failure in the ESV's and B and Aleph's Bibliology. It must be said once again, the Textus Receptus and the King James Version reigns supreme.

h)   *"And no man hath ascended up to heaven, but he that came down from heaven, even the Son of man <u>which is in heaven</u>."* (John 3:13)

Along with P66, 75, B and Aleph, the ESV stumbles at the Lord Jesus Christ's omnipresence. It may be due to the fact that this attribute was veiled during His days amongst us. This is humiliating doctrinal error and blind following of manuscripts B and Aleph. The Textus Receptus and the King James Bible surely deserve to be unsurpassed.

5) Soteriology (Doctrine of Salvation)

a)   *"But go ye and learn what that meaneth, I will have mercy and not sacrifice; for I am not come to call the righteous, but sinners <u>to repentance</u>."* (Matthew 9:13)

The ESV follows B and Aleph in denying the reason for the Lord Jesus Christ's first coming; to call sinners to repentance. This is part of the salvation gospel, and not a call to anything worldly. This is doctrinal failure in this Modern Version (ESV) and leaves the Textus Receptus and the King James Version on top, unequaled.

b)   *"<u>But if ye do not forgive, neither will your Father which is in heaven forgive your trespasses</u>."* (Mark 11:26)

B and Aleph leave this verse out of their manuscripts. Therefore, blindly following, the ESV leave this verse out on forgiveness. We must forgive them. This is doctrinal failure in the Modern Versions and further proves the Textus Receptus and the King James Bible as the best.

c) *"And Philip said, If thou believest with all thine heart, thou mayest. And he answered and said, I believe that Jesus Christ is the Son of God."* (Acts 8:37).

Again, B and Aleph, along with P45 and 74, have come under the knife and this verse is gone from them for evermore. People may be relieved even today who believe in baptism's regenerative powers. This is doctrinal failure in Bibliology as well, proving beyond reasonable doubt of the Textus Receptus and King James Bible superiority.

d) *"In whom we have redemption through his blood, even the forgiveness of sins;"* (Colossians 1:14)

Aleph and Vatican B, along with the ESV delete "through His Blood." We can say we have redemption and forgiveness if the Modern Versions still retain those terms. However, it is always through His Blood that we have redemption and forgiveness. This is obvious doctrinal error in Modern Versions and their underlying texts. The Textus Receptus and the King James Bible will remain theologically unequaled.

No matter all the fanfare and anticipation of the arrival of a new Modern Version on the Christian scene, if it does not prove doctrinally sound it is a dismal failure. Failing to rid the Revised Standard Version of its many shortcomings, the translators could not fashion a trustworthy version in which Bible-believing Christians could place their confidence. All in all, the attempt to turn such a flagging, flagitious version (RSV) into something ostentatious or vivacious was an utter failure.

4. The Contemporary English Version (CEV)

The fourth and final modern Bible Version with its doctrinal failures is the Contemporary English Version (CEV).

To the translators of the CEV, the needs of the hearer are of the primary importance. If you are a reader, that is fine too, since it is implied that today's readers are not familiar with nor are motivated to learn Traditional biblical language.[20]

Perhaps this is the reason that all 29 doctrinal words with the greatest usage and 22 more words of general biblical interest and usage are not found in the CEV.[21]

It seems that this "user-friendly," dumbed down Modern Version was created to set up a parallel universe of Christianity. There is no possibility that anyone spoon-fed this pablum from birth will be able to have any meaningful theological dialogue with a traditionally educated Christian.

Introduction

The Contemporary English Version (CEV) is published by the American Bible Society (ABS). The ABS is one of at least 142 Bible Societies within the United Bible Society (UBS). The UBS distributes millions of Modern Bible Versions yearly throughout the world. It does translation work in hundreds of languages.

The UBS, along with the ABS, has a long, sad history. From its inception, the organization has been permeated with influences from the apostate Roman Catholic Church and apostate Unitarians. The United Bible Society and the American Bible Society are ecumenical in their endeavors. It matters not to them that the Roman Catholic Church preaches a false gospel and is filled with doctrinal errors.

The ABS at a meeting in 1982 had a Roman Catholic speaker and a 7th Day Adventist on a panel. The American Bible Society's "Today's English Version" perversion, published in 1966 gained immediate recognition by the Roman Catholic Church.

Eugene Nida, Father of Dynamic Equivalence Translating Techniques, and former head of the ABS Translation Department, said Roman Catholic work in the ABS was a "very important development."[22]

In 1981, the ABS printed over a half million copies of the "Good News Bible" which had the Apocryphal books included. On October 7, 2008, the ABS presented Pope Benedict XVI with a special Polyglot Bible in five languages, bearing the seals of the ABS and the Vatican.

It is also well known that Cardinal Carlo Martini was an editor of the United Bible Societies Greek New Testament 2nd Edition. We are to be separate from apostates and their works (2 John 8-11). Yet here is such a work by the ABS, the Contemporary English Version.

History

The undertaking that was to become the CEV was begun by Barclay Newman in 1985. It grew out of research with children. Mostly the work was to find out what "street people" were using for language in the 80s and how translating principles could be fashioned accordingly. They studied the language kids were exposed to every day on television, in movies, books, magazines, and newspapers. What people understood the most, what confused them the most, and the language structures that caused the most misunderstanding, were all sorted out and molded into their translation principles. With the help of Eugene Nida and other Bible "specialists" the CEV emerged. The actual work of the translation "is attributed to only three men."[23]

In 1991, the CEV New Testament was released. The CEV Old Testament was completed in 1995, the same year that a complete CEV appeared. The ABS is quick to point out that the CEV is not a revision of the "Good News Bible," but is a fresh translation with a readability level as low as the 4th grade.

Translation Methods

It would not be very hard to guess that the CEV is a solidly Dynamic Equivalent Translation. It simplifies Bible terminology into every day, simple to understand, words and phrases that cannot be done without employing Dynamic as opposed to Formal Equivalency.

Theological terms such as: justification, righteousness, redemption, reconciliation, propitiation, atonement, salvation, sanctification, and repentance are jettisoned. These are given equivalents for clarity of meaning.

The CEV has also eliminated the Words "Lucifer" (Isaiah 14:12) and "Antichrist" from their New Testament. "By using dynamic equivalent wording when speaking of the Greek Words which convey these doctrines, they are either watering down such doctrines or are denying them completely."[24]

By using dynamic equivalents for the 9 theological words they dropped, plus changing 42 other Bible-Church terms and giving absurd reasons for doing so, the CEV translators have become interpreters of God's Words. By avoiding the Formal translation method, the result is a translation that is full of paraphrases and equivalents far beyond anything before the CEV.

Erroneous Hebrew Text

The Hebrew Aramaic text employed is not one that can assure a faithful or accurate English Old Testament. The Hebraica Stuttgartensia of the United Bible Societies was used. The date of that text is 1967/1977. The Hebrew (different from the Hebrew used for the King James Bible) is printed at the top of the page. Footnotes at the bottom of each page correct and change the Hebrew an average of 15 to 20 times per page. This computes to 20,00 to 30,000 changes to the Old Testament. The Stuttgart Hebrew text follows the Ben Asher Masoretic text instead of the Ben Chayyim which underlies the King James Hebrew of the Old Testament. The Stuttgart text follows the Leningrad manuscript (B19 or "L") from 1008 A.D.

Erroneous Greek Text

The CEV translators used the United Bible Societies third edition Greek text, corrected and compared with the Fourth revised edition.[25]

Bruce Metzger himself said that the Nestle-Aland and UBS Committees "began with the Westcott and Hort Greek text" and then they changed parts of it along the way. It is claimed that their Greek texts are not similar to the Westcott and Hort texts, but aside from some minor differences they are virtually identical. This is because they are based on the Gnostic Vatican "B" and the Gnostic Sinai "Aleph" manuscripts. The Textus Receptus underlying the King James Bible differs in over 8,000 places from the UBS Greek 3rd edition.

Doctrinal Failures in the CEV

1) Theology Proper (Doctrine of God).

a) *"And lead us not into temptation, but deliver us from evil: For thine is the kingdom, and the power, and the glory, for ever. Amen*. (Matthew 6:13)

The underlined verse is omitted. This ascribes praise to "Our Father" and is not found in B and Aleph. This doctrinal failure by the CEV does not in any way affect the superiority of the Textus Receptus or the King James Bible.

b) *"Howbeit this kind goeth not out but by prayer and fasting*." (Matthew 17:21)

Aleph and B leave out this verse which denies that God has the power to cast out demons by prayer and fasting. This foundational truth is also omitted by the CEV and proves that the Textus Receptus and the King James Bible are the best.

c) *"And he said unto him, why callest thou me good? There is none good but one, that is, God: but if thou wilt enter into life, keep the commandments*." (Matthew 19:17)

Aleph and B manuscripts again prove themselves deficient by leaving out this underlined phrase. The CEV deletes "good" in verse 16, changing the doctrine that Jesus is God. This proves that the Textus Receptus and the King James Bible are correct and that the CEV has failed in doctrine.

d) "*So the last shall be first, and the first last: For many be called, but few chosen.*" (Matthew 20:16)

Aleph and B, both mutilated manuscripts, leave out "many be called, but few chosen." This mutes the doctrine that God would have all men be saved. The CEV followed Aleph and B and omits this phrase also. This is doctrinal failure and proves the Textus Receptus and the King James Bible as unexcelled.

e) "*And Jesus went into the temple of God, and cast out all them that sold and bought in the temple, and overthrew the tables of the money changers, and the seats of them that sold doves,*" (Matthew 21:12)

This was God's temple and "of God" is left out of the Modern Versions. This depicts that the Lord Jesus Christ, as God, is in the Temple of God, doing the Father's business of restoring the Temple of God to a house of prayer. This is doctrinal failure on behalf of the CEV and proves the Textus Receptus and the King James Bible as unsurpassed.

f) "*Glory to God in the highest, and on earth peace, goodwill toward men.*" (Luke 2:14)

This phrase is missing in Aleph and B and changed to "everyone who pleases God" in the CEV. This affirms that man is somehow good and will be granted peace because of his own merit. This is doctrinal error in the CEV and its underlying corrupted Greek texts. This further proves that the Textus Receptus and the King James Bible are unequaled.

2) Christology (The Doctrine of Christ)

a) "*And knew her not till she had brought forth her firstborn son: and he called his name JESUS.*" (Matthew 1:25)

Here again is the earliest, first mentioned omission of doctrine in the New Testament and it is an important one. The CEV changes "firstborn son" to "her baby" where the idea that

Jesus may not have been Mary's first son and that she could have had other children before Jesus is advanced. The Word "firstborn" does not limit Mary to only one son. This is in direct odds with the Roman Catholic doctrine of Mary's perpetual virginity. This is doctrinal failure in the CEV and in B and Aleph, proving the Textus Receptus and the King James Bible as second to none.

b) *"But be not ye called Rabbi: for one is your Master, even <u>Christ</u>; and all ye are brethren."* (Matthew 23:8)

Aleph and B also are without "Christ." The CEV changes it to Teacher. This affects the doctrine of the Lord Jesus Christ according to His Deity. This is doctrinal error. This bolsters the fact that the Textus Receptus and the King James Bible are the best.

c) *"The first man is of the earth, earthy: the second man is the <u>Lord</u> from heaven."* (1 Corinthians 15:47)

The CEV follows Aleph and B in dropping "Lord" from the verse, thereby trying to remove the deity of the Lord Jesus Christ from the text. This is doctrinal failure in these doctored texts and Modern Versions, adding to the truth that the Textus Receptus and the King James Bible are superior.

d) *"If any man love not the Lord <u>Jesus Christ</u>, let him be Anathema Maranatha."* (1 Corinthians 16:22)

Aleph and B and the CEV drop "Jesus Christ" weakening the Deity of the Lord Jesus Christ. This is doctrinal failure on the part of the CEV and its underlying texts and proves that the Textus Receptus and the King James Bible are unsurpassed.

e) *"Know that he which raised up the Lord Jesus shall raise up us also <u>by Jesus</u>, and shall present us with you."* (2 Corinthians 4:14)

It is the Lord Jesus Christ who will raise us up in the resurrection with bodies to be with Him. This difference makes possible a spiritual resurrection rather than a bodily one for the Lord Jesus Christ and for believers to come. This is doctrinal failure on the part of the Aleph and B Gnostic manuscripts and on the part of the CEV, this furthers the truth that the Textus Receptus and the King James Bible are superior.

f) *"And to make all men see what is the fellowship of the mystery, which from the beginning of the world hath been hid in God, who created all things by Jesus Christ:"* (Ephesians 3:9)

"By Jesus Christ" is not in the corrupted B and Aleph manuscripts and is omitted from the CEV. This is once again an attempt to remove the deity of the Lord Jesus Christ from the Scriptures. Our Lord Jesus Christ was the creator of all things. This is compounded doctrinal failure in the CEV, because of the underlying Westcott and Hort Greek text. This proves to all that the Textus Receptus and the King James Bible are unexcelled.

3) Pneumatology (Doctrine of the Holy Spirit)

a) *"The first man is of the earth, earthy; the second man the Lord from Heaven."* (1 Corinthians 15:47)

Although this verse was covered in the Christology section, there is an application here. The CEV followed Aleph and B in omitting "the Lord" from the verse. But what is not so known is the Gnostic twist that Papyrus 46 gives to the passage; "the second man is the Spirit from heaven." This was the corruption of the 2nd/3rd century Egypt![26] This is clear cut doctrinal failure concerning the Spirit of God. This is the cause of the failure of the CEV and its underlying texts, and proves the Textus Receptus and the King James Bible as the best.

b) *"Seeing ye have purified your souls in obeying the truth through the Spirit unto unfeigned love of the brethren, see that ye love one another with a pure heart fervently:"* (1 Peter 1:22)

B and Aleph are followed again by the CEV while denying the power of the Holy Spirit, for believers to obey the truth. Where that power would come from if it wasn't the Holy Spirit one could only guess. This is doctrinal failure of the false W-H

Greek texts as well as the CEV, conclusively proving that the Textus Receptus and the King James Bible are the best.

4) Bibliology (Doctrine of the Bible)

a) *"That whosoever believeth in him should not perish but have eternal life."* (John 3:15)

The CEV changes this to "son of man" and leaves out any reference to eternal damnation, about which this verse speaks. B and Aleph also change this and are the culprits. You cannot add something and then subtract something from the text, and yet that is what the CEV does. This is doctrinal failure and proves the Textus Receptus and the King James Bible as the most reliable Words.

b) *"For I am not ashamed of the gospel of Christ: for it is the power of God unto salvation to everyone that believeth; to the Jew first, and also to the Greek."* (Romans 1:16)

B and Aleph drop the Words *"of Christ."* The CEV follows suit. The CEV eliminates the doctrinal words "gospel" and "salvation" here and throughout their translation. This is doctrinal failure of the Greek texts underlying the CEV, and doctrinal lunacy on the part of the CEV. This proves that the Textus Receptus and the King James Bible are unequaled.

5) Soteriology (Doctrine of Salvation)

a) *"In whom we have redemption through his blood, even the forgiveness of sins."* (Colossians 1:14)

Here's how the CEV writes this verse: *"Who forgives our sins and sets us free."* (CEV). That is a disgrace. Does that even sound like Bible? The word "redemption" is missing here and throughout the CEV. We are saved and our redemption is made possible through the Blood of the Lord Jesus Christ. The CEV follows Aleph and B in this omission. This is disgraceful doctrinal failure and shows that the Textus Receptus and the King James Bible are unsurpassed.

b) *"Who being the brightness of his glory, and the express image of his person, and upholding all things by the word of his* *power, when he had <u>by himself</u> purged our sins, sat down on the right hand of the Majesty on high;"* (Hebrews 1:3)

Aleph and B have omitted "by himself," negating the fact that the Lord Jesus Christ alone died and purged our sins. Early on in Church history, others were brought into that work which is our Lord's only. The CEV follows right along in this doctrinal failure. There is only one conclusion: The Textus Receptus and the King James Bible are superior.

In conclusion, all of Christendom is worse off for the CEV having been published by the American Bible Society. It is so defective in every way that no biblical Christian should ever go near it. Severe damage will result from the use of this doctrinally failed version.

The same can be said for all four Modern Versions covered in this chapter and the dozens of Modern perversions that are out there. Be smart and continue to use the trusted and faithful King James Bible. It has stood the test of time and will always hold up to the closest scrutiny. Our confidence should be in its superior Hebrew, Aramaic, and Greek Words, the superior translators, its superior translation technique, and its superior theology.

APPENDIX A

"Some Words on Peter Ruckman"

Introduction

In the Bible version war, there are essentially three camps. On the one side are modernist, post-modernist, and very liberal groups and individuals. They form the Translator groups, some within the United Bible Societies, etc. Then there are the Liberal Bible teachers and professors committed to Westcott and Hort, UBS, and Nestle-Aland type Gnostic Hebrew and Greek Words which underlie the Modern Versions. Mainly they believe that God has not preserved His Words for us today.

The next group is the Dean Burgon Society who fights for and defends the traditional Hebrew and Greek Words that underlie our King James Bible. The Dean Burgon Society believes that God breathed out His Words in the Hebrew, Aramaic, and Greek originals. Those Words were preserved in the Masoretic Hebrew, Aramaic, and Received Greek (TR) Words. These reliable, Traditional Texts were then used to translate our King James Bible.

Enter Peter Ruckman

A third party entered into the version issue is the radical heretic Peter Ruckman. He is the one the first group likes to lump the second group into. Dr. Peter Ruckman is a heretic simply for holding radical ideas about God's Words and influencing others with those views that are outside of the Bible.

Dr. Ruckman believes that a translation, such as the King James Bible, can be "inspired," "inspired of God," or "given by inspiration of God." He promotes the idea that God breathed out His Words and they became a perfect King James Bible.

2 Timothy 3:16 says that "*all Scripture is given by inspiration of God*." All (Pasa) Scripture (GraphE) is given by inspiration of God (theopneustos), which are the Words breathed out by God in the Hebrew, Aramaic, and Greek. But the Ruckmanites forcefully project their thinking that God gave a special revelation that is the King James Bible and they wholly ignore the Textus Receptus and Hebrew Words. This leads others to use the depreciatory term "King James only" to describe all those who believe that the King James Bible is the best and most accurate translation. These know-nothings smear members of the DBS and the "Textus Receptus" people with the Peter Ruckman group with this pejorative.

Tenets of Ruckmanism – on Inspiration

The tenets of Ruckmanism, held in common by the members of his organization, separate him from all of Christendom. The first and main pillar upon which all the others are built is that the King James Bible is given by inspiration. All his minions are well versed in preaching inspiration of the King James Bible to any challenger. They parrot the gist of the company line. It goes something like this: "The Bible says, 'all Scripture is given by inspiration.' Therefore, if I quote some Scripture to you, as I just did, it is inspired even when I quote it." Therefore, if it is quoted as Scripture from the King James Bible, then the King James Bible was given by inspiration, or inspired, same thing. Sorry, if something quoted out of the Koran, or the Bhagavad-Gita claims to be given by inspiration, just because it says it is, does not make it so.

On Inerrancy

This leads to another Tenet of Ruckmanism that says the King James Bible is infallible and inerrant. While it is true that the King James Bible is translated from the best underlying Words, those Words represent the inerrant originals that were given inerrantly by the breath of God. No one can give the substance of the attribute of perfection of a Perfect God to a man-written translation, even the King James Bible.

On Preservation

The next tenet of Ruckmanism we are concerned with is the one that says that the King James Bible is the preserved Word of God. Ruckman does believe that the Authorized Version (KJ) is God's Word and he will use the term God's Words, plural, are preserved without any errors in the language which was intended for us, which is English. Ruckman even uses Psalm 12 to prove his theory. But the promise of the preservation of God's Words is contained in the Bible and Psalm 12:6,7 are two verses that prove that. The problem is that those verses in Psalms have nothing to do with the King James Bible. By accepting this tenet of Ruckmanism the door swings open to accept all the other tenets of Ruckmanism. This would be very dangerous and lead one down the path to apostasy by these heresies.

On KJB superior to its underlying texts

Many people are fooled by what Ruckman clearly says about the Hebrew and Greek texts. They think that only the Westcott and Hort type texts are being alluded to. This is not true. He has stated repeatedly that the King James Bible (A.V. 1611) is superior to any Greek text. Listen to him:

> "*The A.V. 1611 text is to be preferred over any Greek text, as it tells the truth of the matter…notice how the English text corrects the errors in the Greek Text.*"[1]

Ruckman believes that the A.V. 1611 is superior in every way, even over the Words from which it was translated. He uses as further proof that the order of the books in the King James is superior to the order of the books in the Hebrew, Aramaic, and Greek Words. What this creates for Ruckmanites is that the only authority for their Christian faith and life is a translation cut free from its moorings. The idiocy of this absurd position is that the Words from which the King James Bible were translated from are inferior to the KJV and the KJV is enthroned to a place of supremacy over them. This opens the door to the heresy that the King James Version contains advanced revelation not contained in the Hebrew, Aramaic, and Greek Words.

On KJV containing Advanced Revelation

The final tenet of Ruckmanism we will be concerned with is the heretical assumption that the King James Bible contains advanced revelation or advanced light. This stance essentially says that you lose light (supposedly spiritual) if you use the Hebrew and Greek Words instead of using the King James Bible exclusively. Listen to Ruckman:

> *"Light is to be found in the Authorized Version text. No other bible* (sic) *contains it. No other translation, of any edition, or in any language (except German) contains this kind of phenomena. If all you have is the 'original Greek' you lose light."*[2]

The reason Peter Ruckman can teach advanced revelation and light for the KJV is that he has magically moved the closing of Scripture Canon by God to 1611. This is truly incredible and unprecedented. Listen to Ruckman again:

> *"The King James Text is the last and final statement that God has given to the world...the truth is that God slammed the*

door of revelation shut in 389 B.C. and
slammed it shut again in 1611."[3]

So, according to Peter Ruckman, God kept the door open to the giving of the Canon for an extra 1500 years and thus the A.V. 1611 is able to boast advanced revelation and give new light. Most all other cults can lay claim to some form of advanced revelation and advanced light through their own writings. If any Christian has entertained any of the teachings of Peter Ruckman, he or she is exhorted to "come out from among them" and separate from this error. A supernatural origin cannot be given to the KJV, it being a human effort of translation, no matter its superior quality, since this is the path that leads to Ruckmanism.

Double Inspiration

Peter Ruckman holds an unorthodox view on double inspiration. By keeping the Canon open until 1611, as he does, is one form of double inspiration. The correct view on inspiration according to the Bible has already been covered. God's breathing out of His Words began with the Old Testament Words and ended between 96–100 A.D.

Ruckman bases his idea on his saying that more than 150 quotes (Scriptures) from the Old Testament appear as a translation in the New Testament. It is his logic that the first time they appeared in the Old Testament, they were "inspired." The next time these same Scriptures appeared in the New Testament, they were "inspired" again. Dr. Ruckman then applies double inspiration to attempt to prove that translations can be inspired. He applies the translation work of the Holy Spirit in these chosen passages, from the Hebrew, Aramaic, and Greek, to man's translation of Bible Versions. To Mr. Ruckman, there is no difference between what the Holy Spirit translates from the Old to the New Testaments, compared to man translating the entire Bible. He also states that the Holy

Spirit, when translating from the Old Testament, does not always translate them literally in the New Testament.

Ruckmanism NOT BEFORE 1950

Dr. R. L. Hymers, Jr., of the Fundamentalist Baptist Tabernacle in Los Angeles, CA has a standing offer of one thousand dollars for anyone who can show that a Baptist or Protestant scholar believed Ruckman's view of an inspired KJV before 1950. Ruckman crows:

> *"The KJV is on par with the originals because it is verbally inspired. No stupid, that is what Christians taught back in 1660-1700, the KJV was directly inspired by the Holy Spirit. He just repeated what was being taught in 1680-1700. I didn't teach that or even imply it."*[4]

This could be Dr. Ruckman's biggest influence over the Church. Too many pastors and teachers have used the terms inerrant, infallible, inspired King James Bible translation. Technically, to be a Ruckmanite you must believe the King James Bible to be inspired. To Ruckman, these are Bible Believers and he must attempt a revision of church history in order to convince his followers that Ruckmanism (belief in an inspired KJV) existed before him.

All of the men that Peter Ruckman praises from the past as holding the position similar to his about the KJV's infallibility, end up upon examination disagreeing with his position. Thus, he ends up bashing present day Believers who hold the same position on the KJV as did the men of previous generations whom he praises.

Peter Ruckman believes that upwards of 40,000,000 Christians are Ruckmanites, those who believe like he does on the inspired King James Bible.

In 1917 W.R. Riley was misrepresented as believing in an inerrant KJV, but he did not believe so. In his book, "The

Menace of Modernism," Riley is quoted: "to claim, therefore, inerrancy for the King James Version or even for the Revised Version, is to claim inerrancy for men who never professed it for themselves."[5]

Ruckman then quotes, in his *"Bible Believers' Bulletin,"* William Lyon Phelps to have held his same position back in 1923. It turns out that Phelps held a "natural inspiration" position and not a "verbal inspiration." Natural inspiration is a position believing that the Bible writers were such genii that they needed no help from God in writing Scripture.

In 1924 Philip Mauro published "Which version? Authorized or Revised." He made this statement: "we do not fail to recognize, what is admitted by all competent authorities, that the A.V. could be corrected in a number of passages…" He did not start the inerrant KJV charge.

In 1925, William Aberhart, author of *"The Latest Modern Movements,"* did not speak of the KJV specifically using terms such as, infallible, perfect, or inspired.

In 1930, Benjamin Wilkenson, a 7th Day Adventist, published "Our Authorized Bible Vindicated." He was crystal clear in denying that any translation could be inspired.

In 1931, William Hoste, in his pamphlet stated that the A.V. was not perfect.

In 1949, though not putting it in print, Ruckman said he came to the conclusion that the King James Bible was infallible and inerrant.

Nowhere is there any hint of anyone up to the 1950's, the mid-fifties, or even into the early 60's professing that the King James Bible was inspired, inerrant, or infallible.

In addition to the 40 million Christians claim, Dr. Ruckman also has attempted to drag Charles Spurgeon, R.A. Torrey, Edward Hills, and Bob Jones, Sr., into his inspired KJV camp. Ruckman has also implied that leaders of the past are partakers in Ruckmanism, including: Oliver Greene, John Bunyan,

Dwight Moody, Billy Sunday, Sam Jones, Gen. William Booth, J. Frank Norris, Dewitt Talmage, and 95% of the members of the ten largest Baptist Churches in America (1970-1985).

Going for the Thousand Bucks

In 1964 Peter Ruckman published *"The Bible Babel."* On page 64 he states; "Alongside the RSV, and ASV, the AV, 1611 is flawless, when it comes to "uniform translating." The floodgates opened.

During the 1960's, the *Bible Believers' Commentary Series* was begun. Its primary purpose was to defend the infallibility of every word of the KJV, something which had never been done before in a Bible Commentary Series.[6]

In 1970, Ruckman wrote the influential book, *"The Christian's Handbook of Manuscript Evidence."* Ruckman begins to hammer hard his theory of the KJV being inerrant and inspired. Dr. Ruckman degrades the use of the Greek in this book, saying on p. 137: *"where the Greek says one thing and the A.V. says another, throw out the Greek."*[7]

In 1973, Bruce Cummons wrote the book, *"The Foundation and Authority of the Word of God."* In it Cummons leaves no doubt as to his belief that we have an infallible translation. Mr. Cummons shows some Ruckmanite influence. He describes Dr. Ruckman as a "thorough student of manuscript evidence." One of the books listed in his Bibliography on the KJV issue, the only one espousing infallibility, was Ruckman's "Christian's Handbook of Manuscript Evidence."

Throughout the 1970's, more and more influence of Ruckmanism shows up in writings. We see writers such as: Herbert Evans, Dick Cimino, Donald Clarke, and references to Ruckmanism in Jack Chick's booklet, "Sabotage?"

Into the 1980's and 1990's, many more writers took a stand for an inspired, infallible, inerrant King James Bible. The influence was by then saturating Christendom.

In the 1980's, we have Ruckman-influenced writers, Homer Massey, Don Edwards, Chester Murry, Barry Burton, Norman Ward, Samuel Gipp, Bob Steward, Robert Sargent, and Michael Breckenridge.

The influence of an inspired KJV continues in the 90's with: James Son, William Grady (*"Final Authority"*), Gail Riplinger (*"New Age Versions," "In Awe of Thy Word"*), and Timothy Morton. Also included, in 1993, is Pastor Mickey Carter of Florida with his tome, *"Things That Are Different Are Not the Same."* On page 74 of that book he says,

> *"The King James Version is the plenary, verbal inspired Word of God. Word for Word, the very minute details (jots and tittles) were God-breathed into man, who wrote it."*[8]

Ruckman kindly refers to Mickey Carter as a friend.

In 1995, Paul Heaton, a pastor in Michigan, published *"What About Those Italicized Words?"* In the second edition (2002) on Page 29, he says:

> *"If any word, or words, in the Authorized King James 1611 Bible are not the inerrant, preserved, inspired* (oops) *Words of God, then pray tell where is that Perfect Bible?"* Heaton recommends further study of Ruckman's "Christian Handbook of Manuscript Evidence."

The Mid-90's continue under the influence of Ruckmanism with writers; Thomas Holland, Michael O'Neal, Roy Branson, James Melton, Ed Devries, and Dr. Soloman Aordkian.

Into the 2000's, we have writers; John Adair, Walter Beebe, Gordon Bane, and Jack Mundey, all towing the line of Ruckmanism.

These writers, and more, from the 1970's up through the present time, all exhibit the influence of Peter Ruckman to one degree or another. Some are very adamant in their belief in an inspired KJV. Even Peter Ruckman is acutely aware of his influence on others.

Michael O'Neal, previously mentioned, summarizes the Ruckman influence of an inspired King James Translation in his book, "*Do We Have the Word of God?*"

> "*And with deepest affection to His servant, Dr. Peter S. Ruckman, who, in my estimation, has influenced more people, directly or indirectly, to believe in the infallibility of their King James Bible, than any other man in the 20th Century.*"[9]

The challenge remains, the thousand dollars awarded to anyone proving that the view of a translation is given by inspiration before 1950 was held by anyone. It is believed that Peter Ruckman will hopelessly continue to name names of those he thinks did agree with his stance. But in every instance he is proven otherwise. It can be stated, as a matter of fact, that no Baptist or Protestant Scholars believed that the KJV was given by inspiration before 1950! However, it is the damaging influence since 1950, introduced by Dr. Peter Ruckman, that the King James Bible translation was given by inspiration and is inspired, inerrant, and infallible that is his biggest blunder. This heresy separates Peter Ruckman and Ruckmanism from the rest of the Christian World. It is a most dangerous heresy that is infecting all of Christendom.

APPENDIX B

Historical Evidences for the Textus Receptus

I quote from *Defending the King James Bible* by Dr. D. A. Waite **(BFT #1594 @ $12.00 + $8.00 S&H)**. He has a section on thirty-seven historical evidences which support the Textus Receptus that underlies the King James Bible. The quotation is found on pages 46-49 of Dr. Waite's book. He wrote as follows:

The Thirty-Seven Historical Evidences Supporting the *Textus Receptus*. Here are the thirty-seven links in the chain of historical evidence to support the *Received Text.*

a.   Historical Evidences for the *Received Text* During the Apostolic Age (33--100 A.D.)

(1) All of the Apostolic Churches used the Received Text.

(2) The churches in Palestine used the Received Text.

(3) The Syrian Church at Antioch used the Received Text.

b.   Historical Evidences for the *Received Text* During the Early Church Period (100--312 A.D.).   Dr. Scrivener and Dean Burgon both agree that, during the first 100 years after the New Testament was written, the greatest corruptions took place to the *Received Text* used by the early church. The B (Vatican) and Aleph (Sinai) manuscripts and the approximately forty-three allies which underlie the Westcott-and-Hort-type text were, I believe, the result of such corruptions. Some of the heretics which operated in this period were Marcion, (160 A. D.); Valentinus, (about 160 A. D.); Cyrinthus, (50-100 A. D.); Sabellius, (about 260 A. D.); and others.

(4) *The Peshitta Syriac Version*, (150 A. D., the second century.) This was based on the *Received Text*.

(5) *Papyrus #66 used the Received Text.*

(6) *The Italic Church in Northern Italy (157 A. D.) used the Received Text.*

(7) *The Gallic Church of Southern France (177 A D.) used the Received Text.*

(8) *The Celtic Church in Great Britain used the Received Text.*

Why did all these have their Bibles based on the Received Text?--the churches in Italy, France, and Great Britain--why? Because those were the true Words of God, **and they knew it**. That was the *Received Text*. They lived in 150 A. D. The Bible was completed in 90-100 A. D. They had the originals right there in their hands and they based it on that which was pure, accurate, and preserved by God and by the Lord Jesus Christ Who preserves everything. These churches used this text and not any other. The heretics made most of the changes in the *Received Text* during this time; the greatest proportion of which, according to both Dr. Scrivener and Dean Burgon, were made during the first 100 years after they were originally written.

(9) *Church of Scotland and Ireland used the Received Text.*

(10) *The Pre-Waldensian churches used the Received Text.*

(11) *The Waldensians (120 A. D. and onward) used the Received Text.*

     c.   Historical Evidences for the *Received Text* During the Byzantine Period (312--1453 A.D.)

     (12) The Gothic Version of the 4th century used the Received Text.

     (13) Codex W of Matthew in the 4th or 5th century used the Received Text.

     (14) Codex A in the Gospels (in the 5th century) used the Received Text.

     (15) The vast majority of extant New Testament manuscripts all used the Received Text. This includes about 99% of them, or about 5,210 of the 5,255 MSS.

     (16) The Greek Orthodox Church used the Received Text. We don't agree with many of their doctrines or practices, but that entire church for over 1,000 years has used the *Received Text.* Why? **They know the Greek language. They're Greeks.** Even though they are **modern** Greeks, they use the New Testament that is based upon the *Received Text* because it is the Words of God, and they know it.

     (17) The present Greek Church still uses the Received Text. When Mrs. Waite and I were in Israel, we visited the church which is supposed to be on the place where Jesus was born, the Church of the Nativity. They have a big Church built on the site. It doesn't look anything like the original place, I am certain. I don't even think it is on the proper place. They have commercialized it. In Jerusalem, they have the Lord Jesus Christ born in various places, crucified in various places, and buried in several places. In the Church of the Nativity, the Lord Jesus Christ's supposed birth place, we met a Greek Orthodox priest. I said to him, "You're a member of the Greek Orthodox clergy, is that right?" He said, "Yes," and then told us his name. I said, "You have a New Testament you use, don't you?" "Oh, yes," he said. I asked, "Which text do you use? Are you familiar with the so-called Westcott-and-Hort-type-text?" "Oh, yes," he said,

"We use the Received Text; we have no confidence at all in the Westcott and Hort text."

That was interesting. The Greek Orthodox Church still goes back to this text that underlies the KING JAMES BIBLE.

d.   Historical Evidences for the *Received Text* During the Early Modern Period (1453--1831 A.D.)

(18) The churches of the Reformation all used the Received Text.

(19) The Erasmus Greek New Testament (1516) used the Received Text.

(20) The Complutensian Polyglot (1522) used the Received Text. A Roman Catholic Cardinal named Ximenes, edited it, yet it was based, **not** on the texts which most Roman Catholic Bibles used, the Westcott and Hort text, but on the *Received Text.*

(21) Martin Luther's German Bible (1522) used the Received Text.

(22) William Tyndale's Bible, (1525), used the Received Text. Tyndale was a great Bible translator who was martyred because of his Bible translation.

(23) The French Version of Oliveton (1535) used the Received Text.

(24) The Coverdale Bible (1535) used the Received Text.

(25) The Matthews Bible (1537) used the Received Text.

(26) The Taverners Bible (1539) used the Received Text.

(27) The Great Bible (1539-41) used the Received Text.

(28) The Stephanus Greek New Testament (1546-51) used the Received Text.

(29) The Geneva Bible (1557-60) used the Received Text.

(30) The Bishops' Bible (1568) used the Received Text.

(31) The Spanish Version (1569) used the Received Text.

(32) The Beza Greek New Testament (1598) used the Received Text. That is the Greek text that the KING JAMES BIBLE was based on, using the 1598, 5th edition of Beza.

(33) The Czech Version (1602) used the Received Text.

(34) The Italian Version of Diodati (1607) used the Received Text.

(35) The KING JAMES BIBLE (1611) used the Received Text.

(36) The Elzevir Brothers' Greek New Testament (1624) used the Received Text.

(37) The Received Text in the New Testament *is* the Received Text--the text that has survived in continuity from the beginning of the New Testament itself. It is the only accurate representation of the originals we have today!

In fact, **it is my own personal conviction and belief, after studying this subject since 1971, that the WORDS of the Received Greek and Masoretic Hebrew texts that underlie the KING JAMES BIBLE are the very WORDS which God has PRESERVED down through the centuries, being the exact WORDS of the ORIGINALS themselves**. As such, I believe they are **INSPIRED WORDS**. I believe they are **PRESERVED** WORDS. I believe they are **INERRANT** WORDS. I believe they are **INFALLIBLE WORDS**. This is why I believe so strongly that any valid translation MUST be based upon these original language texts, and these alone!

APPENDIX C

The King James Bible with Good Doctrinal Fruit
And the Modern Bible Versions with Evil Doctrinal Fruit

I wanted to illustrate the "Good Doctrinal Fruit" of the King James Bible as well as the "Evil Doctrinal Fruit" of modern Bible versions. To do this, I asked Dr. D. A. Waite if I could use the pictures in his *Defined King James Bible* in my book. He said that I could.

The pictures on the following pages are slanted due to the way they were scanned from the *Defined King James Bible*. Despite this, I hope that the charts will illustrate the doctrinal purity of the King James Bible as well as the doctrinal impurity of in more than 356 New Testament passages in the following modern Bibles, just to name a few:

1. The Good News Bible (GNB)
2. The New American Standard Version (NASV)
3. The New English Bible (NEB)
4. The New International Bible (NIV)
5. The Revised Standard Bible (RSV)
6. The New Revised Standard Bible (NRSV)
7. The Today's English Bible (TEV)

For a list of all 356 New Testament doctrinal passages where these modern Bibles are doctrinally in error, along with the Greek manuscript evidence for each, you can consult *Early Manuscripts, Church Fathers, and the King James Version* **(BFT #3230 @ $20.00 + $8.00 S&H)** by Dr. Jack Moorman.

1694   *The Defined King James Bible*

GOOD FRUIT

KJB
Holy Bible

EVERY VITAL
DOCTRINE PRESERVED

Deity of Christ

Virgin Birth of Christ

Redemption by the
Blood of the Lamb

GOOD TREE

GOOD TRANSLATORS	GOOD TECHNIQUE
GODLY MEN	FORMAL EQUIVALENCE

GOOD TEXT
TEXTUS RECEPTUS

"... every good tree bringeth forth good fruit."
Matthew 7:17

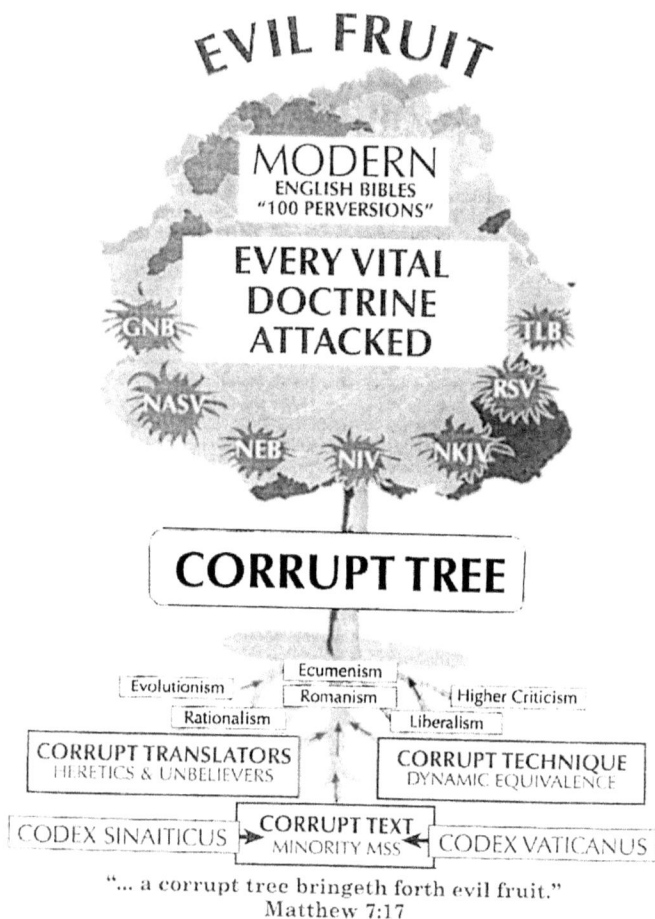

EVIL FRUIT

MODERN
ENGLISH BIBLES
"100 PERVERSIONS"

EVERY VITAL DOCTRINE ATTACKED

GNB   TLB   NASV   RSV   NEB   NIV   NKJV

CORRUPT TREE

Ecumenism
Evolutionism   Romanism   Higher Criticism
Rationalism   Liberalism

CORRUPT TRANSLATORS
HERETICS & UNBELIEVERS

CORRUPT TECHNIQUE
DYNAMIC EQUIVALENCE

CODEX SINAITICUS   **CORRUPT TEXT** MINORITY MSS   CODEX VATICANUS

"... a corrupt tree bringeth forth evil fruit."
Matthew 7:17

END NOTES

Introduction
1. Hillary Clinton, *Senate Committee Hearing on Benghazi*, January 23, 2013.

Chapter 1
1. II Corinthians 10:4-6.

Chapter 3
1.Reno, Paul J. *Sincerity*, Paper given at DBS, July 2010.

Chapter 4
1. *Dean Burgon Society News*; any issue.
2. Waite, *DBS News*, issue 107, p. 4.
3. Hort. *Life*, Vol 1, p. 416.
4. Westcott. *Life*, Vol 1. p. 78.
5. Hort. *Life*, Vol 2, p. 50.
6. Westcott. *Life*, Vol 1, p. 81.
7. Waite. *Defending the King James Bible*, p. 40.
8. Khoo, Jeffrey. *Kept Pure in All Ages*, p. 60.
9. *Dean Burgon Society News*.
10. Waite, Dr. D. A. and Yvonne S. *Who Was Dean John Burgon?*, p. 5.
11. *Ibid*, p. 7.
12. Waite. *Defending the King James Bible*, p. 40.
13. *Ibid*, p. 41.
14. Burgon, Dean. *Revision Revised*, p. 301.
15. Moorman, Dr. Jack. *Early Manuscripts*, p. 26.
16. *Ibid*. p. 26.
17. Waite. *Defending the King James Bible*, p. 48.

Chapter 5

1. #3-6 of the *DBS Articles of Faith.*
2. Hymers, Dr. R.L. *Ruckmanism Exposed*, Introduction.
3. *Ibid.* p.5.
4. *Ibid.* p. 6.
5.Waite, Dr. D.A. *The Meaning of Biblical "Inspiration,"* B.F.T. #2237-T, pp. 2, 3.
6. *Ibid.* p. 3.
7. Burgon, Dean. *Inspiration and Interpretation*, p. 76.
8. Strouse, Dr. Thomas. *The Translation Model Predicted*, 5 paragraphs.
9. Lampe. *The Forbidden Book*, p. 36.
10. Waite. *The First 200 Questions Answered*, p. 6.
11. *Ibid.* p. 6.
12. *Dean Burgon Society Articles of Faith, Bible.*
13. *DBS Questionnaire/Application.*
14. *Inspiration and VPP.* www.BibleForToday.org/VPP_Course/Lesson_2. htm. p. 3.
15. *Ibid.* p. 4.
16. Rockwood, Perry. *The Inspired King James Bible.* Gospel Standard. 5-2001. p. 5.

Chapter 6

1. Wallace, Daniel. *The Majority Text Theory.* Journal of Evangelical Theological Society (Jets), p. 16.
2. *Ibid.* p. 1.
3. DiVietro, Dr. Kirk. *Preservation of God's Words*, p. 3.
4. Wallace, *Majority Text Theory*, p. 1.
5. Burgon. *The Traditional Text*, p. 13.
6. Waite. *Defending the King James Bible.* pp. 8-9.
7. *Biblical Support for the Doctrine of VPP.*, Lesson 4. www.BibleForToday.org/VPP_course/lesson.
8. Waite. *Fundamentalist MIS-information.* p. 9.

9. *Ibid.* p. 55.

10. *Ibid.* p. 55.

11. Waite. *Fundamentalist Deception on Bible Preservation.* #28 and #31. DBS Paper. 7-2004.

12. Waite. *Bob Jones University's Error on Bible Preservation* Statements #18 and #20 and #21. pp. 11-13.

Chapter 7

1. Lampebroadcast.org. *Law of First Mention.* Reprinted by the OldPathsPublications.com.

2. Barnard, Richard K. *God's Word in Our Language: The Story of the New International Version.* Grand Rapids, MI 1989. p. 18.

3. Waite, Dr. D. A. *Defects in the New International Version.* B.F.T #2054. Collingwood, N.J. p. 7.

4. *Ibid.* p. 7.

5. NIV. *Preface.* pp viii-ix.

6. Trinitarian Bible Society. *The NIV.* p. 14.

7. Waite. *Defects in New International Version.* p. 8.

8. NIV. *Preface.* p. viii.

9. Waite. *Defects.* p. 9.

10. Williams, Dr. H. D. *Word-For-Word Translating.* 2007 p. 4.

11. Williams. *Word-For-Word Translating.* Quoting Eugene Nida in *Translating Truth.* pp. 53-54.

12. Cloud, David W. *Encyclopedia of the Bible and Christianity.* Ontario, Canada. 1997. p. 122.

13. NASV. *Preface.* p. viii.

14. Wallace, Daniel B. *Mark 1:2 and New Testament Textual Criticism.* 1997.

15. *Ibid.* p. 2.

16. ESV. *Title Page.* Backside.

17. Waite. *Defending the King James Bible.* p. 95.

18. Williams. *Word-For-Word Translating.* p. 60.

19. ESV. *About the ESV.* pp. 221-222.

20. Paraphrased from CEV's *Introduction.*

21. Waite. *The Contemporary English Version.* pp. 15-16.

22. *Calvary Contender.* Sept. 1992.

23. Bible Researcher. *The Contemporary English Version.* p. 2.

24. Waite. *Contemporary English Version.* p. 7.

25. CEV. *Preface.* p. xxiii.

26. Moorman. *Early Manuscripts.* p. 252.

Appendix A

1. Ruckman, Dr. Peter. *The Christian's Handbook of Manuscript Evidence.* p. 124. Quoted from Hymers, *Ruckmanism Exposed.* p. 9.

2. Ruckman. *The Christian's Handbook of Biblical Scholarship.* p. 336. Quoted in *Ruckmanism Exposed.* Hymers. pp. 10-11.

3. Ruckman. *The Monarch of the Book!* p. 9. Quoted. *Ruckmanism Exposed.* p. 11.

4. Ruckman. *The Last Grenade*, p. 261. Quoted. Ruckmanism.org.

5. Quoted from, *Ruckmanism Exposed.* Hymers. p. 59.

6. *Who was First Prominent KJV Defender to Influence Others?* Ruckmanism.org.

7. *Ibid.*

8. *Ibid.*

9. *Ibid.*

BIBLIOGRAPHY

Books

Bancroft, Emory H. *Elemental Theology*. Kregel Publication. Grand Rapids, MI. 1996.

Barnett, Robert J. *The Word of God on Trial*. Revival Literature. Ashville, NC. 2007.

Bennett, David C. *God's Marvelous Book–The Bible*. Bible for Today Press, Collingswood, NJ. 2-2013.

Brandenburg, Kent. Editor. *Thou Shalt Keep Them*. Pillar & Ground Publishing. El Sobrante, CA. 2003.

Brown, Dr. David L. *Understanding the Battle Over Bible Versions*. FBC Publications. Oak Creek, WI. 2010.

Clarke, Adam. *Commentary of the Bible*. Abridged by Ralph Earle. Baker Book House. 1985.

Cloud, David W. *Way of Life Encyclopedia*. Oak Harbor, WA. Way of Life Literature. 2nd Edition. 1997.

DiVietro, Dr. Kirk D. *Preservation of God's Words*. B.F.T. #2772. July, 1997.

Gurnall, William. *The Christian in Complete Armour*. Volumes I & II. Banner of Truth Trust. 1864.

Hymers, Dr. R. L. Jr. *Ruckmanism Exposed*. Fundamentalist Baptist Tabernacle. Los Angeles, CA. 1998.

Khoo, Jeffrey. *Kept Pure In All Ages*. Far Eastern Bible College Press. Singapore. 2001.

Kirszner and Mandell. *The Holt Handbook*. Harcourt Brace College Publishers. 5th Edition. FL. 1999.

Lampe, Dr. Craig. *The Forbidden Book*. 2004.

Lockyear, Dr. Herbert. *All The Doctrines of the Bible.* ZonderVan Publishing House. Grand Rapids, MI. 1964.

MacArthur, John. *The Believer's Armor.* Moody Press. Chicago. 1981.

Moorman, Dr. Jack A. *Early Manuscripts, Church Fathers, and The Authorized Version.* Bible For Today Press. Collingswood, NJ. July, 2005.

_____ *Missing in Modern Bibles.* B.F.T. #1726. Collingswood, NJ. 1989.

_____ *Three Hundred and Fifty-six Doctrinal Errors in the N.I.V. and Other Modern Bible Versions.* B.F.T. #2956. Collingswood, NJ. 1990.

Phillips, John. *Bible Explorer's Guide.* Kregel Publications. 1987, 2002.

Ray, Jasper James. *God Wrote Only One Bible.* EyeOpener Publications. Eugene, OR. 1983.

Sizemore, Denver. *13 Lessons in Christian Doctrine.* College Press. Joplin, MO. 1981.

Smith, Randy. *Theologicalisms.* Countryside Institute For Biblical Studies. Southlake, TX. March, 2000.

Stringer, Dr. Phil. *The Scripture Cannot Be Broken.* Faith Baptist Publishers. Ft. Pierce, FL. Date unknown.

Strouse, Dr. Thomas M. *The Lord Hath Spoken: A Guide to Bibliology.* Tabernacle Baptist Press. Virginia Beach, VA. 1992.

Unger, Merrill F. *Ungers Bible Dictionary.* Moody Press. Chicago. 1973.

Vance, Laurence M. *Double Jeopardy: The New American Standard Bible Update.* Vance Publications. FL. 1998.

Waite, Dr. D.A. *The Contemporary English Version (CEV): An Antichrist Version (ACV)?* B.F.T. Press. Collingswood, NJ. 1996.

_____ *The Case for the King James Bible*. B.F.T. Press. Collingswood, NJ. 2001.

_____*Defending the King James Bible*. B.F.T. Press. Collingswood, NJ. 1998.

_____*Fundamentalist Mis-information on Bible Versions*. B.F.T. Press. Collingswood, NJ. 2000.

_____*Fundamentalist Distortions on Bible Versions*. B.F.T. Press. Collingswood, NJ. 1999.

_____*Bob Jones University's Errors on Bible Preservation*. B.F.T. Press. Collingswood, NJ. 2006.

_____*The Superior Foundation of the King James Bible*. B.F.T. Press. Collingswood, NJ. 2008.

_____*Brief Analysis of the N.I.V. Inclusive Language Edition*. B.F.T. #2768. Collingswood, NJ. 1997.

_____*A Critical Answer to James Price's King James Onlyism*. B.F.T. Press. Collingswood, NJ. 2009.

Williams, Dr. H. D. *The Miracle of Biblical Inspiration*. The Old Path Publications, Inc. Cleveland, GA. 2009.

_____*Word-For-Word Translating of the Received Texts*. B.F.T. Press. Collingswood, NJ. 2007.

Wilmington, H.L. *The Complete Book of Bible Lists*. Tyndale Publishers. Wheaton, IL. 1987.

ARTICLES

Anderson, G. W. & D. E. *What Today's Christian Needs to Know About the N.I.V.* Trinitarian Bible Society. 1992.

Bible Study Guides. *The Belt of Trust*. Lesson 2, www.freebiblestudyguides.org/bible-teachings/armor-of-god-bi blestudy.

Biblical Research Studies Group. *The Law of First Mention*. www.biblicalresearach.info/page48.html

Blann, Rusty. *Casting Down Imaginations*. S.O.A.P. for Today. 2009.

Blanton, Raymond. *The Promise of Preservation.* B.F.T. #1622.

Bloomer, George. *Casting Down Imaginations.* Bethel Center. 1999.

Cloud, David. *Biblical Inspiration.* Way of Life. 2007.

_____ *Why I have Not Signed the New DBS Statement.* Fundamentalist Baptist Information Service. Aug, 2003.

_____*The United Bible Societies and Rome.* www.wayoflife.org/database/ubandrome.html Nov, 2008. pp. 1-8.

Corbett, Andy. *Ten Lessons on English Composition.* Macedonia Baptist College.

David, Mr. *Who Was the First Prominent KJV Defender to Influence Others to Declare the KJV to be Inerrant or Inspired in the 20th Century?* www.ruckmanism.org/firstinfluence. pp 1-46.

Decker, Dr. Rodney J. *The English Standard Version: A Review Article.* Journal of Ministry & Theology. Fall, 2005. pp. 5-26.

Doom, Dr. Robert. *An Evaluation of the Contemporary English Version.* Presented at DBS Meeting. July, 1992l *Inspiration and VPP.* www.biblefortoday.org/VPP_counse/lesson_2htm pp. 1-4. *Inspiration and VPP.* www.biblefortoday.org/VPP_counse/lesson_4htm pp. 20-24.

Jack, Danny. *The Superiority of the King James Bible.* Guiding Light Baptist Church. Nova Scotia, Canada.

Jasmin, Dr. Don. *Fundamentalist Citadel Approves NCCC Based Spin-off Bible Version.* Fundamentalist Digest. June, 2004. pp. 21-30.

Khoo, Jeffrey. *Inspiration, Preservation, and Translations.* Far Eastern Bible College.

LampBroadcast.org. *The Law of First Mention.* Reprinted by OldPathsPublications.com/.../Law%20of%20first%20ment ion.pdf.

Living Word Library. *The Belt of Truth.* August 15, 2009. www.wordlibrary.co.uk/article.php?id=98

Moehlenpah, Arlo E. *Casting Down Imaginations.* Doing Good Ministries. 2001.

Paisley, Dr. Ian. *The Contemporary English Version Bible; The Latest in the Perversion of the Scriptures.* www.ianpaisely.org. pp. 1-7.

Reno, Paul J. *Sincerity.* Given at DBS meeting. July, 2010.

Reynolds, Jr. M. H. *Casting Down Imaginations.* Foundation Magazine. 2013.

Simpson, Andy. *How to Prepare a Thesis.* Carolina Bible College.

_____*Ten Lessons on English Composition.* Macedonia Baptist College

Straub, Jeff. *How a Translation Became a Litmus Test for Theology.* Baptist Bulletin. July, 2011.

_____ *KJV Only?*
http://baptistbulletin.org/?p=16763. Pp 1-5

Stringer, Dr. Phil. *The Canon of Scripture.* pp. 1-3.

Strouse, Dr. Thomas. *But My Words Shall Not Pass Away; the Biblical Defense of the Doctrine of the Preservation of Scripture.* Tabernacle Baptist Press. Virginia Beach, VA.

_____*Psalm 12; 6,7 and The Permanent Preservation of God's Words.* Emmanuel Baptist Seminary. pp. 1-3.

Vance, Laurence M. *The NRSV vs The ESV.* Vance Publications. pp. 1-6.

Waite, Daniel S. *What is Truth?* Dean Burgon Society Messages. July 14-15, 2010. pp. 40-46.

Waite, Dr. D.A. *The Meaning of Biblical Inspiration.* The Bible For Today. #2237-T. 1992.

_____*Fundamentalist Deception on Bible Preservation.* Paper at DBS meeting. July, 2004. p. 129.

_____*Defects in the New International Version.* B.F.T. #2054. 2013.

_____*The Definition of Bible Preservation.* Paper given at DBS meeting. July, 2012. pp. 115-121.

Waite, Dr. D.A. and Yvonne S. *Who was Dean John Burgon?* Bible For Today. Collingswood, NJ. B.F.T. #2839.

Waite, Yvonne S. *B.F.T. Update: March-April 2013.* The Bible For Today Ministries. pp. 1-7.

Wallace, Daniel B. *The Majority-Text Theory: History, Methods, and Critique.* Journal of Evangelical Theological Society. June 1994. pp. 185-215.

Wardrobe From the King. *Clothed with Truth.* www.crossroad.to/bible_studies/wardrobe/chapter2.html

Wikipedia, The Free Encyclopedia. *New International Version.* en.wikipedia.org/wiki/new_international_version.

Winograd, Robert. *Evolutionary Semantics Version.* DBS Annual Meeting. July, 2010. pp. 1-10.

Wright, Kim. *Casting Down the Imagination.* Free Publishing Guide.

Index Of Words And Phrases

.

Modern Version Failures

By Charles Kriessman

Background of Modern Versions.

This book gives a brief history of the original language texts. It presents the failure of the Gnostic Critical Greek Texts of the New Testament as well as the superiority and excellence of the Traditional Received Greek Words which underlie the King James Bible. The reason for so many doctrinal failures in the modern Bible versions is because they have been based on the fraudulent Greek Vatican and Sinai manuscripts which are loaded with over 356 false doctrinal passages.

Modern Versions Analyzed.

The modern versions which are briefly analyzed for doctrinal failures are: (1) The New International Version; (2) the New American Standard Version; (3) the English Standard Version; and (4) the Contemporary English Version. Each of these versions is an example of the doctrinal errors that are to be found in the many other versions which are also founded on the erroneous Gnostic Critical Greek Texts.

Errors of Peter Ruckman.

Appendix A explains that the King James Bible is not "inspired" in any way. Only the Hebrew, Aramaic, and Greek Words that God gave us have been "inspired" or God-breathed. Peter Ruckman and his many followers and partial followers are refuted in this error.

www.BibleForToday.org

BFT 4085   **ISBN #978-1-56848-097-8**

www.ingramcontent.com/pod-product-compliance
Lightning Source LLC
LaVergne TN
LVHW021457080426
835509LV00018B/2314